POSITIVE

ACCOUNTABILITY

FOR TEAMS

Other books by April Sabral

The Positive Effect for Retail Leaders
Incurable Positivity
Incurable Positivity Workbook and Journal
The Positive Effect for Education
Live Purposely, Lead Positively Workbook

More resources:

The Positive Effect Podcast
Incurable Positivity Podcast
Deck of Inspiration

Positive Accountability

Table of Contents

Table of Contents

Introduction

Picture a Starbucks near Miami Beach with sunburnt tourists shuffling up to the counter at 15th and Ocean Drive. I was the store manager back then, hustling through endless orders of macchiatos and frappuccinos. The place never slowed down. It always looked like an airport terminal. A large percentage of the guests were on vacation, snapping photos with their drinks like they were souvenirs.

But there was one problem, and it drove us crazy: drinks kept vanishing off the bar. Not because we weren't making them—but because the wrong hands kept grabbing them. Tourists, in their flip-flops and beach tans, would waltz up, snag the first beautiful, blended thing they saw, and float off like it was no big deal. It didn't matter if it was cold brew or chai latte—if it looked frosty and sweet, they claimed it. Meanwhile, the rightful owners would stand there fuming: "Where's my drink?" Complaints stacked higher than the whipped cream tower on a venti mocha.

Our customer satisfaction scores tanked, and I'll admit—I wanted to blame the crowd. After all, how do you manage chaos when the chaos doesn't care? But our district leader wasn't having it. She looked at us and said, "Stop pointing at the tourists. What can you own? How can you fix it?"

That word—own—hit differently. Accountability wasn't about guilt; it was about agency. So, instead of shrugging at the madness, my team and I put our heads together and thought about the process. We asked: How do we outsmart confusion? How do we make sure the right drink lands in the right hand?

The solution was laughably simple: write the customer's name on the cup. But we developed it into our style. Sharpie, big letters, bold and personal. No more guessing. Every cup found its rightful owner.

Almost overnight, the complaints stopped. Tourists didn't care if their name was misspelled; they liked the personalization. Locals cared that they walked away with the drink they'd actually ordered. Our scores rose. Our waste from remakes dropped. Customers felt seen. And without realizing it, we'd sparked a practice that would grow into one of Starbucks' signature moves around the world.

Positive Accountability

It started as a problem to be solved. It ended as a lesson in accountability: when you take ownership of the problem, you don't just protect the customer experience—you can change an entire culture. And everyone wins.

That's the thing about accountability. When someone makes the decision to say, This is ours to solve, the company wins, the employees win, and the customers win!

Accountability. The word itself can evoke a range of emotions—apprehension, frustration, curiosity, or even confusion. It carries weight, often associated with blame, punishment, or micromanagement. But in reality, true accountability is none of those things. In fact, when utilized correctly, it's not negative at all. It's positive! It is a tool for development.

In the context of leadership and team dynamics, accountability is the cornerstone of positive results and award-winning success. It has been the energy of high-performing teams in my time leading, the driving force behind innovation, and the foundation upon which trust, transparency, and sustainable growth are built.

Accountability is not about assigning blame or pointing fingers. It's about transforming accountability into a positive force that empowers individuals, strengthens teams, and drives exceptional results. It's about cultivating a culture where people take ownership of their actions, contribute their best work, and collaboratively strive toward shared goals, without fear or hesitation, and step into their best selves, it's about leaders bringing out the best of their team and honoring their word.

But understanding the "why" behind accountability is only half the battle. The real challenge lies in the "how." When I ask leaders in conferences, team meetings or one-on-ones what accountability is? I get a multitude of answers. This in

When people ask me, I say it's a nine-step framework that cultivates positive leaders, teams, results and a winning culture and most of all clarity.

itself creates confusion. Leaders tell me it's managing people's performance and having tough conversations. They are right. This is a part of accountability for sure. But there is so much more.

Accountability is a nine-step framework that cultivates positive leaders, teams, results, a winning culture, and most of all clarity. What I have learned by leading, coaching, and managing teams along with training and coaching leaders through some of their toughest challenges is that the more you define what accountability is and explain it in a framework that everyone understands, it becomes less about a tough conversation and more about a culture of progress.

That's why this book isn't just a theoretical exploration; it's a practical guide, structured around our comprehensive nine-step framework that will help you build a truly accountable, high-performance culture. Each step is carefully explained, supported by proven tools, techniques, and real-world examples to guide you through the mindset shifts and strategic actions and skills that are necessary for lasting transformation. True accountability is not a vague conversation; it is much more than that. And over the years I've heard from leaders how it has impacted their leadership.

Just last week I was in a conference and ran into a leader who had attended one of our workshops over four years. He said that he'd used step number three just yesterday, and it makes all the difference to how his team responds and takes action. He said it was one of the most effective frameworks he'd ever learned and

You will gain access to our Accountability Index **for FREE** so that you and your team can assess your level of accountability and identify where you have room to grow. My hope is that you will take this to heart, implement what you've learned, and watch your culture transform.

Now, you may be wondering if I'll bring AI into this book. Yes, but the focus here is not on educating you about AI or technology. In a world where technology is rapidly replacing jobs and conversations lean toward innovation, I wrote this book for *human leaders* to strengthen their *human skills*.

That said, as we think about accountability, there are three skills every team must build to thrive in the next era of work: **curiosity, ideation, and agency.** These are not just buzzwords; they are the foundation of ownership and accountability.

Building accountability in your team requires building their skills. If you approach AI (and other tools) purely from a *skill-building perspective* and then transfer the ownership to your team to master these three skills, your team will become unstoppable.

The 9-step accountability wheel is a framework that is truly transformational. This is not AI; it is purely human capital management.

In this book, we will also address the skillset required to acquire accountability, offering practical guidance for effective communication, performance management, and conflict resolution. You'll find actionable checklists, concise summaries, and case studies designed to help you apply these principles in real time, no matter your industry, leadership level, or organizational size.

Throughout these pages, we will explore the critical distinction between responsibility and accountability, what I have learned through leading hundreds of teams and training leaders within large and small organizations. I'll dispel common myths and misconceptions that often hinder its effective implementation.

Many organizations believe that accountability simply means ensuring people do what they're told but true accountability goes much deeper than task completion. We will uncover the tangible benefits of an accountable culture, from increased productivity and profitability to improved morale and enhanced employee engagement and positivity. YES, positivity. If I am writing a book, it <u>has </u>to include positivity. Accountability is one of our core pillars in The Positive Effect Training. Without it leaders struggle to build teams who take ownership and responsibility. Knowing how important this skill is, we decided to write an entire book dedicated to just accountability. Below you can see the six drivers of positive leaders. One being the Ownership & Accountability Driver.

Positive Accountability

Performance & Growth Manager

Relationship Builder

Coach & People Developer

Positive Effect Leaders

Positive-Intent Communicator

Ownership & Accountability Driver

Mindset & Energy Steward

This diagram is taken from The Positive Effect Leadership System (TPE). If you are ready to get started, we are ready to teach you. Thank you for caring enough to read and develop your skills.

Chapter 1: Beyond Blame & Responsibility – The True Power of Accountability

That night, standing in front of the mirror, it hit me: if I couldn't get over my fear of conflict and start having courageous conversations, I would continue to hold my team back. And worse, I was about to derail my career.

It was a hard pill to swallow.

I wanted to progress. I wanted to provide a better life for my kids. I wanted that next role, and I wanted to earn more. That meant taking a long, hard look at my leadership and asking myself what needed to change.

I called them uncomfortable back then because I had not yet developed the skills to give my team fearless feedback and have honest conversations. I had to make a choice: was I going to let fear derail my career, my goals, and my dreams? Or was I going to be comfortable being uncomfortable? I had to ask myself what I wanted and what I was willing to do to get it. On the other hand, I had to ask what the impact would be on the team if I didn't.

Have you ever delayed giving feedback to someone knowing full well you owed it to them to be honest and direct? Maybe a direct report, a boss, a peer, or even a partner that you wanted to say something to but didn't feel safe or comfortable enough to say it? We've all been there. But why?

Humans are hardwired to avoid conflict. Our brains protect us from anything that feels like danger. And giving feedback, saying what you need to, does not always seem easy. Nobody really wants to tell another person that what they are doing isn't great. Nobody truly wants to go into a situation that they feel could become confrontational.

In my experience leading and working with others for over three decades, the conflict we create inside ourselves to avoid conversations that are necessary is an inner turmoil. It is based on the wrong belief that holding our people accountable is dangerous and destructive to high performance.

But providing feedback isn't about conflict; it's about care. It's about helping someone else step into their potential, just as much as it's about helping yourself step into yours. When you understand this perspective and reframe conflict to care, it becomes easier to hold a team accountable.

The Leaders Who Changed Everything

I've been fortunate to work under two specific leaders who truly stood out amid many. These two leaders demonstrated what positive accountability looked and felt like—and the benefit of working for such leaders set me up for significant growth, not only in my leadership but in my entire life. They weren't just "managing" people or "enforcing rules." They created an environment where I felt empowered to take full ownership of my work.

When I succeeded, they celebrated. When I made mistakes, they coached me through them, helping me improve without shame or blame. Their leadership style gave me the confidence to take risks, think independently, and grow into my role far faster than I would have under fear-based leadership. They were kind, clear, and focused. They operated without judgment and had this innate ability to have honest conversations that motivated me to deliver exceptional results, make behavioral changes, and grow.

That experience shaped my philosophy and became the foundation of The Positive Effect Transformational Programs, which I now teach to global organizations. I've seen firsthand what happens when accountability is approached positively and with a clear framework—people thrive, teams perform, and businesses grow. I've also seen it from the other side of the coin: fear and control.

I am sure you, too, can think of a leader who demonstrated positive accountability—someone who didn't just hold you responsible but helped you step up, learn, and achieve more than you thought possible. There are many incredible leaders out there who lead this way, yet the challenge lies in teaching and developing it across teams and entire organizations.

Silos Erode Shared Responsibility.

Many times, silos appear in companies. 83% of companies report that silos exist within their organization. 97% of those say these silos have a negative effect on company performance. When departments or teams operate in silos, they focus on their own goals instead of the organization's bigger mission. This weakens accountability because people can say, "That's not my problem, it's theirs." If accountability becomes part of your culture, it shifts from being a task or policy to being a shared mindset. People no longer view accountability as "something leadership enforces" but as "how we do things here." *A silo refers to a situation where people, teams, or departments within an organization operate in isolation instead of collaborating. Information, goals, and resources get trapped within one group, making it harder for others to access or contribute.*

Imagine if accountability could become like your vision and mission statement—a part of how you operate daily? A way of living and a way of doing business. The goal of this book is to provide you with the words, frameworks, and strategies to demystify accountability so it can be deeply ingrained in your company's culture—not through fear, but as a motivating, inspiring, positive, and powerful tool for growth.

True accountability is not about control—it's about creating an environment where people take ownership because they want to, not because they're afraid not to. When accountability is done right, it fuels engagement, strengthens trust, and unlocks extraordinary results. It has a positive effect on teams and results. In the pages ahead, we'll embark on a journey together—a journey toward building a culture where accountability isn't just a word, but a way of life. A culture where leaders empower, teams thrive, and success follows naturally.

Beyond Blame and Responsibility

I remember clearly a leader I once worked for who made me fearful of coming to work. She was someone who, I believe, meant well, but her approach to leadership created an environment where positive accountability couldn't thrive. Instead of empowering her team, she micromanaged every detail, watching over us with a critical eye, ready to pounce on any mistake.

At the peak of the discomfort, we were asked to recite a script verbatim in a regional meeting at a round table with twenty other leaders present. It was a clear indicator to me that trust and coaching skills were nonexistent. In this environment I remember constantly feeling judged, overwhelmed, and afraid of making even the smallest misstep. It wasn't just me—our entire team operated in fear. Meetings were tense, conversations were guarded, and innovation was nonexistent. We weren't focused on solutions or results, we were focused on avoiding blame.

This experience taught me a powerful lesson: blame kills accountability. It creates a culture where people play it safe, avoid risks, and stop taking ownership of their work. And without ownership, there's no accountability.

When I led teams at DAVIDsTEA, we strived to build the opposite of a blame culture. We trained employees to own the customer experience not just to sell tea, we wanted our teams to create a journey of discovery for every customer that was engaging and exciting. The teams were empowered to make decisions in real time, solve problems, and deliver exceptional service. This sense of ownership transformed our teams into high-performing, results-driven powerhouses. We focused on setting clear positive outcomes and allowed our teams to take ownership of how they got there.

The difference between these two cultures is night and day. One stifles growth, the other fuels it. As leaders, we have a choice: do we create a culture of fear, or do we create a culture of positive accountability?

Recognizing the difference between blame and responsibility was a defining moment in my growth. It was like flipping a switch. I realized that owning my journey wasn't about avoiding failure—it was about stepping up, learning, and continuously getting better.

The empowering leaders I worked for lit the path forward for me. They made growth feel attainable. They showed me that accountability isn't about being perfect; it's about being present, proactive, and willing to stretch. Even the leaders who instilled fear gave me a positive gift: the gift of what not to do.

Have you ever felt like this? The dreaded walk to a meeting, or an email that evoked negative emotions and stress? We all have. As you read on, I want you to think about moments in your career where you may have caused unnecessary stress due to a lack of process that could empower your team. It is in the self-awareness of leadership the moments we are not proud of that we can grow into the leaders our teams need us to be.

You see, as a leader, your role is to inspire, motivate, transfer ownership, and create a safe space for your team to experiment with responsibility. Without this, they will lack the confidence to explore possibilities that may be far beyond your capabilities and vision.

Removing blame is a superpower for organizations to build positive accountability. When this happens, teams become unstoppable in their pursuit of meaningful experiences, products, and results that fuel profitability. When leaders say things like, "I have to do everything because my team does not step up" or "I can't pay what other companies pay," I hear excuses and blame. When leaders talk about their team like this, it destroys positive culture and motivates team members to resign and work somewhere else.

The Ripple Effect of Leadership

By modeling accountability, leaders create a ripple effect that influences teams, business culture, and individual growth. The most powerful question every leader should ask themselves is this: What kind of ripple effect am I creating today with my team, peers, and customers? And own it. Because whether it's positive, negative, or neutral, you are the one who creates this. And when you realize and take ownership and responsibility, providing honest conversations doesn't feel so hard.

I've seen firsthand how one leader's actions can set the tone for an entire organization. Let's talk about this for a moment, because taking your part in what could be your own lack of accountability is the first step. If you read the first book I ever wrote, *The Positive Effect*, you will remember the famous one million dollar chocolate bar story. I have told this story over and over during trainings and keynotes. It is a powerful story because there are so many lessons in it. But I think the number one take away that every leader remembers is the power of taking responsibility.

I call it the "One million dollar chocolate bar" story where I learned the importance of my role as a leader. Lack of ownership could have derailed my entire team in their quest to reach a goal of one million in sales that we had been asked to achieve. I had to admit that my limiting beliefs were not going to lead my team across the finish line. So, I took ownership, reset the course, and went to work to make it happen. Nobody had to tell me what to do; the sense of ownership kicked in. We surpassed the goal with flying colours.

Imagine if I had blamed the company for giving me such high goals and went down the road of complaining about my leaders to anyone who would listen. How could we have achieved our sales goal with that kind of flawed leadership on my part?

When leaders demonstrate accountability by admitting mistakes, owning outcomes, and focusing on solutions it inspires their teams to do the same. This ripple effect doesn't just stop at the team level, it extends to customers, stakeholders, and the broader community. Leading by example is a key component to transform a team from it's not my problem to how do we fix this?

Accountability as a Competitive Advantage

When implemented correctly, accountability creates a culture where individuals are motivated to do their best work, learn from failures, and contribute to collective success.

I've said it before and I want to say it again because it's important: Accountability is not about punishment; it's all about clarity, combined with ownership, commitment, and growth. When implemented correctly, it creates a culture where individuals are motivated to do their best work, learn from failures, and contribute to collective success.

Organizations that embrace accountability as a core value see tangible benefits:

- Higher employee engagement: People feel connected to their work when they understand their role in the company's success.
- Lower turnover rates: When employees feel supported and responsible for their growth, they are less likely to leave.
- Improved collaboration: Accountability fosters open communication and teamwork, as individuals understand how their contributions impact others.

The Nine-Step Framework for Positive Accountability

Throughout this book, I'll introduce you to a nine-step framework designed to help leaders and teams build a culture of accountability. This framework isn't just theoretical; it's practical, actionable, and proven to drive results.

Together, we'll explore:

- The role of psychological safety in fostering accountability.
- How open, positive, and supportive communication builds trust and encourages ownership.
- The importance of a growth-oriented mindset and learning agility in teams.
- Practical strategies for setting clear expectations and holding teams accountable.
- Real-world examples of organizations and leaders that have mastered accountability to drive performance.

This framework will provide you with the tools to demystify accountability, making it a natural and valued part of your organization's culture.

Building a culture of accountability is not a one-time event it's a continuous process that requires commitment, flexibility, and open collaboration. By focusing on five key areas;:

❖ Transparent communication

- ❖ Involving employees in the process
- ❖ Continuous feedback and adaptation
- ❖ Psychological safety and a growth mindset
- ❖ Recognizing and rewarding accountability

When leaders can turn accountability from a task into a mindset team members feel engaged and empowered, when this happens, accountability becomes a natural and valued part of the culture, not something imposed from above. With the right approach, accountability ceases to be a challenge and becomes the driving force behind a high-performing, resilient, and motivated team.

Accountability as Transformation
True accountability doesn't just improve individual performance; it transforms teams, strengthens organizations, and drives long-term success.

Accountability as Transformation

True accountability doesn't just improve individual performance, it transforms teams, strengthens organizations, and drives long-term success. As you continue reading, you'll discover practical steps, real-world examples, and actionable strategies to make accountability a cornerstone of your leadership and culture. Let's embark on this journey together and unlock the true power of accountability.

Self-Reflective Questions for Leaders

To close this chapter, I want to leave you with some thought-provoking questions to reflect on. These are designed to help you evaluate your leadership style, your approach to accountability, and the ripple effect you're creating within your team. Take some time to consider these, and if possible, write down your answers. Self-reflection is the first step toward meaningful growth.

Think about a time when you felt empowered by a leader. What specific actions or behaviors made you feel that way? How can you replicate those behaviors with your team? Reflect on a moment when you avoided taking accountability for a mistake. What held you back? How could you have approached the situation differently? When was the last time you celebrated a team member's success? How did it impact their confidence and performance? Consider a time when your team missed a deadline or failed to meet expectations. How did you respond? Did your response encourage ownership, or did it create fear?

How often do you seek feedback from your team about your leadership style? What have you learned from their input, and how have you acted on it? Think about a recent challenge your team faced. Did you focus on finding solutions, or did you spend more time identifying who was at fault?

What kind of ripple effect are you creating today with your team, peers, and customers? Are you modeling the behaviors you want to see in others? Reflect on your communication style. Are you clear and consistent in setting expectations, or do you assume your team understands without confirming?

When was the last time you admitted a mistake to your team? How did they respond, and what did you learn from the experience? If your team were to rate your accountability as a leader, what score do you think they would give you? Why?

These questions are not meant to criticize but to inspire growth. The more self-aware you become, the more effectively you can lead with accountability, empowering your team to thrive.

Chapter 2: Driving Results and Growth

Why Accountability is the Key to Growth

In the previous chapter, we explored the core of accountability—how it goes beyond responsibility and is not about blame but ownership. Now, it's time to examine why accountability is the single most important factor in driving business growth, performance, and results.

Think about this: McKinsey's research shows that companies with clear accountability and healthy organizational practices generate *three times the total shareholder return* compared to those that don't. That's not a small difference—it's the line between thriving and merely surviving. They also found that when leaders establish real role clarity—when everyone knows who owns what—organizations are nearly *five times more likely* to be healthy and deliver results.

Accountability is very much about leadership. But it's also a powerful strategy.

In other words, accountability isn't just a "nice-to-have leadership trait." It's the backbone of performance.

Businesses that embed accountability into their culture not only grow faster but also keep their people longer, with turnover rates dropping and revenue growth rising by as much as 30%. Contrast that with companies that avoid accountability: confusion grows, silos deepen, and results stall.

So, when we talk about accountability as the engine of growth, it's not theory—it's proven practice. The numbers make it clear: organizations that practice accountability outperform those that don't.

Accountability is very much about leadership. But it's also a powerful strategy. Another study published in Harvard Business Review found that companies with strong accountability cultures experience a 20% increase in profitability compared to organizations that lack it. This is not a coincidence. When employees feel accountable for outcomes, they take initiative, problem-solve, and find ways to be more effective without waiting for permission.

When teams work in an environment of shared accountability, they don't waste time blaming or finger-pointing, they focus on solutions and results. When leaders model accountability, they inspire a culture where everyone owns their success, raising the bar for performance across the organization.

Let's dive into the real-world impact of accountability on results and growth. One of the biggest benefits of accountability is supercharged productivity—not just "doing more" but working smarter, more efficiently, and with purpose.

I remember when I led retail stores, I saw a clear difference between stores that embraced the accountability wheel and those that didn't. The most successful stores had a culture of ownership. Employees were empowered to make decisions that drove sales and customer satisfaction, even when the leaders weren't there.

What makes a team or store embrace accountability? And others don't? Leadership. We focus so much on process, operations, standards, SOPs and other technical things a business requires to operate. But leadership and lack of it is the number one driver of a team's overall mission and determines how they drive the business. When leaders understand that the magic of creating an accountable team is training and development along with specific steps that are transparent to everyone involved, they move beyond their own limitations and get courageous. This is when it transfers. Of course, hiring well is important. But I have seen low performing teams move from mediocre to high performance in 30 days with a new team leader who implements the accountability framework you are going to learn about today.

At DAVIDsTEA, accountability wasn't just a concept—it was lived out daily. We didn't simply train employees to sell tea; we developed them to *own* the customer experience. That meant guiding customers through every step of their journey, transforming a simple purchase into an educational and enjoyable exploration of tea. That's why we called them Tea Guides.

One regional director really embodied this ownership mindset. She didn't wait for instructions; she created opportunities. She organized tea tastings in busy mall corridors during peak hours, partnered with other retailers by giving out tea coupons, and found ways to bring tea into people's hands before they even set foot in the store. It worked so well that her approach was rolled out nationally— a perfect example of how accountability fuels innovation and growth.

This culture of accountability showed up in individual stores too. I'll never forget one location in Vancouver. The team there fully embraced the Nine-Step Positive Accountability Wheel as soon as it was introduced. They weren't just following steps; they were taking ownership. They offered recommendations, solved customer problems in real time, and made sure every interaction was exceptional. The results spoke for themselves: five-star reviews across the board and sales consistently outperforming other locations.

The lesson here is simple: when you set clear expectations, provide the right tools, and empower people to act, accountability turns into ownership—and ownership drives results.

On the other hand, I've shopped in stores where it's evident the team is not empowered to make decisions. One such experience was in Toronto, where I tried to make a simple purchase. The employee at the register had no authority to resolve an issue. They had to call a manager for approval—

for something as minor as a price adjustment. The manager, in turn, seemed reluctant to take ownership, bouncing the issue to someone else. The entire experience felt disorganized, slow, and frustrating. I wasn't surprised when that company eventually closed its North American operations—a lack of accountability at every level cripples a business.

Recently, I ordered a salad in a local healthy lunch spot and asked for the red onions to be on the side instead of on the salad. The employee said, "We cannot do that." I asked for her manager who said, "Oh, head office won't let us do that." After a very awkward conversation about my simple request and two managers later, my lunch companions and I decided to leave and go to a different location to grab lunch. Whenever I am in these situations, it makes me wonder whether head office knows the amount of times this happens in a day and that their policies derail the happiest and most positive customer from buying.

This happens across all areas of businesses, not just in retail. Organizations with managers who empower employees with accountability move faster, operate smarter, and create better customer experiences—which leads to greater revenue and success. One of the first things we did when I was a field recruiter at Apple was to introduce a survey post interview/hiring seminars to gather feedback on the hiring experience.

Why was this important? Because I remember the candidates experience being subpar based on how the leaders showed up to hire. With a survey in place, even if the candidate did not get hired we were measuring experience, this gave me something tangible to hold the leaders accountable to. Setting clear expectations and then having a metric which was candidate satisfaction was helpful, this shifted the results and immediately influenced the hiring decisions.

Organizations with managers who empower employees with accountability move faster, operate smarter, and create better customer experiences—which leads to greater revenue and success.

No longer could we say "you're not a fit." We had to actually quantify it and ensure that even if they were not hired, they had a stellar experience. The lesson in this was that as soon as we put some KPI and structure involved in our measuring strategy, results, we had a huge improvement and filled over four hundred roles that we had been struggling to fill.

How Apple Built Accountability into its DNA

Accountability isn't just about individual productivity—it's about team success. Few companies understand this better than Apple.

Apple is known for its high-performance culture, and at the heart of this success is its Directly Responsible Individual (DRI) model—a system that ensures clear ownership at every level. At Apple, no task is assigned to a vague team. Instead, every major component of a project—whether it's a new iPhone feature, MacBook redesign, or iOS software update—is owned by one clearly identified person.

This means:

- ❖ No confusion over who's responsible for what.
- ❖ No endless back-and-forth over decision-making.

❖ Every individual knows exactly what they are accountable for.

The DRI model allowed Apple to move faster, maintain quality, and innovate ahead of competitors. When Apple was developing the first iPhone, Steve Jobs didn't just assign a massive team to "figure it out." Instead, he broke the project down into highly accountable teams, each responsible for a core component—like the touchscreen interface, App Store, and camera system.

Because each team knew they owned the outcome, they operated at a level of precision and efficiency that led to one of the most groundbreaking products in history. The takeaway? Accountability is what turns ideas into results.

Accountability Creates Engaged, High-Performing Employees.

Beyond productivity, accountability is a game-changer for employee morale. People want to work in environments where they feel trusted and valued and what is expected and measured, they want to have clarity.

When employees feel that their work matters, and understand what's expected, and even more importantly what happens if they don't meet expectations, they:

- Feel more engaged in their roles.
- Take greater pride in their work.
- Stay longer with the company, reducing turnover.

Early in my career, when I worked at Starbucks, I saw this in action. Starbucks had a "Just Say Yes" policy—an accountability-driven approach that empowered every employee, even part-time baristas, to solve customer problems without waiting for a manager.

I remember one instance when a customer spilled his drink right after receiving it. Instead of waiting for approval, the barista immediately made him a new one, free of charge. This small but powerful authority makes employees feel more confident and engaged, and it made a huge difference in customer satisfaction. It's accountability in action.

Companies like Netflix take this idea even further. Netflix's "freedom and responsibility" model gives employees autonomy over their work. They don't have rigid office hours, vacation policies, or micromanagement—just clear expectations and high accountability.

This creates a culture where:

- Employees take full ownership of their roles.
- There's no need for micromanagement.
- Performance is measured by results, not just effort.

As a result, Netflix has one of the most innovative, high-performing teams in the world. When employees feel trusted to be accountable, they don't just show up for work—they fully engage with it.

Self-Reflective Questions for Leaders

To help you link your team's results to their behavior and the correlation between clear expectations and outcomes, here are some self-reflective questions:

- Have I clearly communicated expectations to my team? How do I know they understand them?
- When results aren't met, do I focus on the process or the person?
- How often do I validate that my team knows their goals and how to achieve them?

- Have I created a culture where employees feel safe to take ownership of their work?
- Do I model accountability in my own actions and decisions?
- When was the last time I provided feedback that was both constructive and empowering?

- How do I respond when mistakes are made? Do I coach through them or assign blame?
- Have I set up systems or frameworks, like the nine-step accountability wheel, to guide my team?
- Do I celebrate and recognize employees who demonstrate accountability?
- How do I ensure that my team feels confident and equipped to make decisions in my absence?

Why Accountability is the Ultimate Growth Strategy.

The difference between a thriving company and a struggling one often comes down to accountability. Organizations that embed accountability into their culture experience:

- Higher productivity and efficiency.
- Stronger teamwork and collaboration.

- More engaged, motivated employees.
- Faster innovation and problem-solving.
- Greater financial performance.

Accountability is a skill that can be built, nurtured, and developed. In the next chapter, we'll explore exactly how to implement accountability in your own organization—turning these insights into action.

Because in today's world, accountability isn't just a competitive edge—it's the foundation for lasting success.

Chapter 3: Navigating Change and Complexity

The Role of Supportive Leadership in Accountability

In this chapter, we'll explore how leaders can be supportive while still holding their teams accountable. In *The Positive Effect for Leaders*, I introduce a strategy that begins with acceptance and why this mindset is critical to accountability.

Here's the truth: leaders who struggle with acceptance often fall into a false belief—that you can't be both supportive *and* hold people accountable. But in reality, support doesn't mean lowering standards or avoiding tough conversations. Support means accepting people's differences, being open to their feedback, and recognizing their limitations while still guiding them forward.

This distinction matters. When the Nine-Step Positive Accountability Wheel is introduced from a place of support, it becomes a tool for growth and ownership—not a form of punishment.

I've heard countless leaders wrestle with this balance. They'll say things like, "It's *hard to be tough*" or "*Don't be too nice.*" But neither extreme creates a healthy, supportive culture. The real power comes when leaders embrace both: offering genuine support while holding their team accountable to the standards that drive results.

I once coached a district manager who admitted she avoided addressing performance issues because she "didn't want to hurt people's feelings." Her team liked her, but they weren't improving, and her results lagged behind other regions. Together, we worked on shifting her mindset from "being nice" to *being supportive through acceptance*. She began acknowledging her team members' efforts and challenges while also setting clear expectations and following through on accountability. Within months, her results turned around, and her team reported feeling more motivated—not less—because they finally knew where they stood and what was expected of them.

Just recently, I interviewed an author on the power of empathy in leadership. She shared that being kind versus being nice is a clear way to think about empathy. I agree with this. You can hold people accountable, be kind and supportive while, not having to worry about being nice.

ACCEPT and the Six Supporting Blocks of Change

The six supporting blocks of change—Vision, Skill, Incentives, Resources, Communication and Feedback, and Action Planning, are all supporting you to build a higher level of positive accountability.

I agree with this. You can hold people accountable, be kind and supportive, not having to worry about being nice.

Supportive leaders who navigate change effortlessly use the six support blocks intermittently with the nine step positive accountability framework. When aligned with the ACCEPT mindset, they provide a comprehensive approach to leading through change. Let's explore how the six pillars of positive change relate to accountability.

Vision

Without a clear vision, employees feel confused. Leaders must ACCEPT the reality of the situation and articulate a compelling purpose for the change.

Example: When I led a team of 200 stores, we set a vision to improve sales by focusing on daily goals. This clarity inspired alignment and accountability.

Skill

Lack of skill creates anxiety. Leaders must ACCEPT that employees have different strengths and provide training to close gaps.

Practical Tip: Offer workshops or coaching to build confidence and competence.

Incentives

Without motivation, employees feel resistance. Leaders must ACCEPT that recognition and rewards drive engagement.

Practical Tip: Celebrate wins publicly to reinforce positive behaviors.

Resources

Lack of resources leads to frustration. Leaders must ACCEPT the need to provide tools and support for success.

Practical Tip: Use project management tools to streamline workflows and ensure transparency.

Action Plan

Without a roadmap, employees feel overwhelmed. Leaders must ACCEPT the importance of breaking down goals into manageable steps.

Practical Tip: Summarize key takeaways and next steps at the end of meetings to ensure alignment.

Accountability

Without accountability, employees feel complacent. Leaders must ACCEPT the need to set clear expectations and follow through.

Example: I remember taking over the field team at DAVIDsTEa and having to figure out how to set clear expectations around cultivating a performance driven culture, this culture meant that we had to deliver sales results not just positive experiences. It came to my attention that many stores were missing the goal by under $50 a day. When you add that up, it can cost the company millions. We gathered together and I asked my team to just start with one simple change: they called a store or walked into one, I challenged them to ask, "What's your sales goal today?"

(Obviously, after we'd said hello and how are you today.) But this slight shift in how they started the conversations created a culture of accountability and improved performance across 200 stores. Why? It put a clear expectation on every multi-site leader that they had to include that question into their first five minutes of every interaction, this translated into results matter to 200 plus stores. We improved sales almost instantly.

I remember a time when I wasn't clear with my vision, and it caused confusion within my team. I was leading a group of multi-site leaders, and we were rolling out a new operational strategy. I assumed they understood the "why" behind the change, but I hadn't communicated it effectively. As a result, they were hesitant, unsure of how to implement the strategy, and morale dipped.

When I finally sat down with them, I realized the issue wasn't their resistance—it was my lack of clarity. I hadn't shared the vision in a way that connected with them. Once I explained the purpose and how it would benefit their teams, the energy shifted. They felt empowered, and the strategy was implemented successfully.

Today, I see similar confusion in organizations around AI. Employees fear it will take their jobs, and without clear communication about how AI will enhance the workplace, that fear grows. Supportive leadership is key to cultivating change and accountability in these moments. A supportive leader would have a clear communication strategy and know exactly who on the team needs to hear what to empower them to move ahead willingly.

The Connection Between ACCEPT, the Six Blocks, and Psychological Safety

Psychological safety is the belief that employees can speak up, admit mistakes, and share ideas without fear of punishment or judgment. It's a critical component of accountability, and it starts with acceptance.

When leaders align ACCEPT with the six supporting blocks, they:
- Create clarity and purpose through Vision.
- Reduce anxiety by building Skill and providing Resources.

- Foster engagement with Incentives and an Action Plan.
- Drive ownership and results through Accountability.

On the flip side, when any of these blocks are missing, negative emotions—confusion, anxiety, resistance, frustration, or complacency—can derail progress.

Practical Strategies for Practicing ACCEPT and the Six Blocks

Ask, Don't Assume.

When faced with a challenge, ask questions to understand the other person's perspective.

Acknowledge Differences.

Adapt your leadership style to meet individual needs.

Celebrate Mistakes as Learning Opportunities.

Focus on what can be

learned rather than assigning blame.

Model Acceptance.

Show your team that it's okay to admit mistakes and give feedback.

Align the Six Blocks.

Regularly assess whether Vision, Skill, Incentives, Resources, Action Plan, and Accountability are in place.

By integrating a supportive approach with the six supporting blocks of change, leaders can create a culture where accountability is empowering, not intimidating. This approach fosters trust, adaptability, and engagement, enabling teams to navigate complexity and achieve their full potential.

As you move forward, ask yourself:

- How can I align the six blocks with the ACT framework taken from The Positive Effect System, in my leadership?
- What assumptions or judgments do I need to let go of?
- How can I create a no-judgment zone for my team?

By embracing acceptance and aligning the six blocks, you'll not only strengthen accountability but also inspire your team to thrive in times of change.

The six blocks of change from The Positive Effect Leadership System.

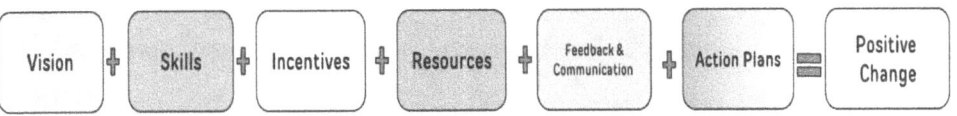

Chapter 4: Evaluating Your Leadership Style and Accountability Practices

Before you can build a culture of accountability, you first need to understand your leadership style and how it influences accountability within your team. This is not about self-criticism or pointing out flaws. It's about self-awareness and growth. It's about identifying what's working, what's not, and where there's room for improvement.

Think of this process as a leadership checkup. Just like a professional athlete reviews their performance after every game, leaders must regularly assess their approach to accountability to ensure they are setting their teams up for success. Too often, when accountability issues arise, leaders focus on fixing employees.

They ask questions like:

- Why are my team missing deadlines?
- Why aren't they taking initiative?
- Why do they avoid responsibility?

But what if the real issue isn't your team? What if it's you. Great leaders understand that accountability starts at the top. This chapter will guide you through a structured process of reflection, assessment, and action. It will help you pinpoint strengths in your leadership style, uncover blind spots, and develop a roadmap for strengthening accountability.

Great leaders understand that accountability starts at the top.

By the end, you'll not only understand your current approach to accountability but also have concrete strategies to enhance it—ensuring that your team operates with clarity, ownership, and confidence.

The Power of Self-Assessment in Leadership Growth

Leadership isn't about having all the answers—it's about having the self-awareness to ask the right questions. Many leaders assume they are fostering accountability, but in reality, their behaviors may be unintentionally undermining it.

If your team struggles with consistently missed deadlines, a lack of initiative or ownership, hesitation to speak up or share ideas, Or poor follow-through on tasks, then, it's time to look inward and ask:

- Am I clearly communicating expectations?
- Do I create a culture of trust, support, and accountability?
- Do I lead in a way that enables or hinders my team's ability to take ownership?

When accountability is lacking in an organization, it's rarely just an employee issue; it's a leadership issue. Employees model their behavior after their leaders. If leaders hold themselves accountable, teams will follow. But if leaders avoid responsibility, blame others, or micromanage, employees will either become fearful and disengaged or passive and complacent. The best way to build an accountable team is to first build an accountable leadership style.

How Do You Communicate Expectations?

- One of the biggest reasons accountability falls apart is because expectations were never truly set in the first place. Think about the last time you delegated something important.
- Did you tell them the goal, the deadline, and the deliverables—or did you just give a quick direction and move on?
- Did you explain *why* the task mattered and how it connected to the bigger picture—or assume they already knew?
- Did you pause to check for understanding—or assume silence meant agreement?

Here's the truth: most leaders believe they're being clear, but in reality, they're only half-communicating. They hand off a task and walk away, only to return later wondering, *"Why didn't this turn out the way I wanted?"*

The missing piece? Testing for understanding. Most employees will not stop you to ask for clarity—they'll nod politely, walk away, and then try to figure it out on their own. And that's when accountability breaks down.

Clear expectations aren't about saying something once. They're about making sure your team heard it, understood it, and knows exactly what success looks like.

Case Study: Howard Schultz, Starbucks CEO When Howard Schultz returned to Starbucks after stepping away, he found the company had lost sight of its core mission. Sales were declining, the brand was becoming diluted, and employee morale was low. His first priority? Clarify expectations. Schultz redefined Starbucks' core values, re-communicated what excellence looked like, and ensured that every employee from baristas to senior executives understood their role in delivering a great customer experience.

This renewed clarity reignited accountability at every level of the company, driving Starbucks back to growth.

Reflection Exercise:

Think of a time you assigned a task that didn't go as planned. Write down exactly how you communicated the assignment.

_____

_____

_____

_____

_____

_____

_____

Now ask yourself: Would this have been clear if I were the one receiving the instructions? If the answer is no, this is an opportunity for improvement.

3 Steps to Set Expectations That Stick

1. **Define It Clearly**

   State the goal, timeline, and deliverables in plain

language. Don't assume they'll fill in the blanks.

2. **Connect the Dots**

   Explain *why* the task matters and how it ties into the bigger picture. People commit more when they understand the purpose.

3. **Check for Understanding**

   Ask them to recap what they heard. This isn't about testing—it's about alignment. Most employees won't ask for clarity, so you must create the space for it.

When you slow down to follow these three steps, accountability speeds up.

How Do You Handle Feedback & Mistakes?

A leader's reaction to mistakes determines whether employees own their failures or hide from them.

- Do you provide consistent, constructive feedback that helps employees grow?
- Do you recognize both effort and results?

- When mistakes happen, do you focus on blame or solutions?

Case Study: Satya Nadella, Microsoft CEO

When Satya Nadella became CEO, Microsoft was struggling with internal competition, fear-based leadership, and a lack of accountability. Employees were hesitant to take risks because failure often resulted in criticism or punishment. Nadella recognized this as an opportunity to shift Microsoft's culture fundamentally by embracing the principles of a growth mindset, a concept introduced by psychologist Carol Dweck.

Dweck defines a growth mindset as believing one's abilities and intelligence can develop through effort, learning, and persistence, rather than being fixed traits. Nadella applied this idea by encouraging employees to view failures not as setbacks, but as valuable learning opportunities that drive innovation and improvement. Under his guidance, employees were empowered to experiment, learn openly from mistakes, and share knowledge freely without fear.

This cultural shift dramatically improved morale, collaboration, and innovation, transforming Microsoft into one of the most agile, accountable, and innovative companies in the world.

To demonstrate a growth mindset here are some self-reflection questions to ask yourself:

- How do I react when someone on my team makes a mistake?
- Do I encourage a problem-solving mindset, or do I focus on fault-finding?
- When was the last time I gave constructive feedback to someone?

If mistakes are met with fear, accountability will suffer. But if they are treated as learning opportunities, accountability will flourish.

Are You a Micromanager or Too Hands-Off?

Finding the right balance between structure and autonomy is critical for building accountability.

Ask yourself:

- Do I frequently check in on small details, making my team feel controlled?
- Or do I step back so much that my team feels directionless and unsupported?

Case Study: Steve Jobs, Apple CEO

Steve Jobs was renowned for his exceptionally high expectations combined with an empowering leadership style. He consistently encouraged his teams to push boundaries and innovate, giving them ownership over their projects while clearly defining essential standards and expectations. Jobs understood that innovation thrives within clear guidelines, where employees feel free to experiment but remain aligned with a cohesive vision.

The key to Jobs' leadership was striking a careful balance between providing freedom and maintaining structure. By clearly communicating non-negotiable core values and objectives, he fostered an environment where creativity flourished. Teams knew precisely what was expected of them, allowing them to focus their energies on developing groundbreaking products.

This approach significantly contributed to Apple's phenomenal success, leading to iconic innovations such as the iPhone, iPad, and MacBook. Jobs' leadership style not only drove Apple to become a leader in technology but also set a standard for cultivating innovation and accountability within the broader tech industry.

Practical Reflection:

- Identify one area where you over-manage or under-manage.
- Adjust your approach to allow more autonomy or provide more clarity.

It's time to assess your accountability. Your Leadership Accountability Scorecard.

Use the following self-assessment to reflect on your leadership style. Rate yourself from 1 (Strongly Disagree) to 5 (Strongly Agree).

✓ I clearly communicate expectations and timelines for all projects.

✓ I provide regular, constructive feedback to my team.

✓ I create a psychologically safe environment for open communication.

✓ I empower my team members to take ownership and responsibility.

✓ I focus on solutions rather than blame when addressing mistakes.

✓I actively solicit feedback from my team members.

✓I regularly review and adjust my accountability practices.

✓I lead by example, demonstrating personal accountability.

What Your Scores Mean:

4-5: Strong accountability practices. Keep refining them.

2-3: Areas for improvement. Choose one to work on first.

1: Critical area needing immediate attention.

Leadership Growth Through Accountability

When you hold yourself accountable to a higher standard, your team will naturally follow. The next step? Commit to reflection, seek feedback, and start implementing small but meaningful changes.

You can head to:

https://www.positiveaccountability.info/

 Take the accountability INDEX for free. And see in more detail where your opportunities are.

Chapter 5: Understanding the Perspectives of All Involved Parties

In this chapter, we will explore the critical role of alignment in cultivating a robust culture of accountability. Strong accountability is rooted in clear, consistent expectations, both internally within the organization and externally with stakeholders. Achieving this alignment requires active engagement with all relevant parties, ensuring everyone's perspectives are heard, acknowledged, and effectively integrated. By bridging internal and external expectations, organizations can foster greater trust, collaboration, and collective commitment to shared goals.

Moving beyond the internal dynamics of your team, the next critical step in assessing your accountability landscape is to consider the broader ecosystem of stakeholders.

Accountability isn't confined to the walls of your department or team; its impact ripples outward, affecting clients, senior management, cross-functional teams, and even the organization as a whole. To create a truly effective and sustainable accountability framework, understanding the perspectives of all involved parties is essential. Ignoring these external viewpoints risks creating a system that works well internally but clashes with the expectations and needs of those outside your immediate team. This can lead to conflict, frustration, and ultimately, a breakdown in accountability.

Identifying Key Stakeholders in Accountability

A comprehensive stakeholder analysis involves systematically identifying all individuals or groups affected by, or invested in, your team's performance and accountability practices. This isn't just about listing names it's about deeply understanding their unique perspectives, expectations, and concerns.

For example:

- Team members may view accountability as a system of control or a tool for growth.
- Senior management often sees accountability as a mechanism for ensuring project delivery and achieving strategic goals.
- Clients or customers prioritize quality, reliability, and responsiveness.

Each of these perspectives must be acknowledged and balanced to build an effective accountability culture.

Let's explore these stakeholder groups in more detail.

1. Understanding Your Team's Perspective

Accountability starts with your people. It assesses how your team *perceives* accountability and whether they see it as a positive path to growth or as a heavy set of rules will determine how they engage with it. If they see it as empowering, they'll lean in. If they see it as restrictive, they'll pull back.

So, how do you get real insight into what they're thinking? Don't just rely on performance reviews or hallway chats. Mix it up:

- Run a quick, anonymous pulse check (Shorter is better. Three sharp questions can tell you more than a ten-page survey).
- Host informal roundtables or "listening huddles" where people feel safe to share what's really happening on the floor.

- Sit down one-on-one and simply ask, *"What's helping you take ownership right now? What's getting in the way?"*

Questions like these open the door:

- Do you feel accountability is applied fairly across the team?
- Are there areas where you feel stretched too thin or unsupported?
- What would help you step up and own your role with more confidence?

When you start asking and really listening, you shift accountability from a top-down demand into a shared agreement. The message becomes clear: *we're in this together, and accountability is about helping you succeed, not catching you fail.*

2. How Clients and Customers Experience Accountability

Accountability doesn't stop at the team room door; it spills directly into how clients and customers experience your business. The question is: do they feel like they can count on you?

Customers don't just buy products or services; they buy promises - promises of quality, responsiveness, and timeliness. If those promises are broken, trust erodes. Accountability is the glue that keeps those promises intact. Think about it:

- Do your clients know exactly what to expect from you?
- When things shift (because they always do), does your team proactively communicate the change, or do clients discover it on their own?

- Are there clear ways for clients to share feedback and actually see it acted on?

Here's the litmus test: if customer complaints are recurring—say, delays, missed details, or inconsistent service that's often a signal your internal accountability is off track. Maybe resources aren't allocated properly, maybe commitments are fuzzy, or maybe communication breaks down.

The solution? Flip the script. Build external accountability through transparency:

- Run short client surveys or quick pulse-check calls.
- Hold regular check-in meetings not just when things go wrong.
- Share progress updates openly, even when the news isn't perfect.

When clients see you consistently owning the process, whether outcomes are good or bad, they trust you more. Accountability, in their eyes, becomes reliability.

3. How Senior Leaders View Accountability

Now let's flip the lens upward. Senior management looks at accountability differently. They're not as focused on the daily grind they're focused on the bigger picture:

- Are we hitting strategic goals?
- Are financial and operational targets on track?

- Can we trust the data we're seeing to make decisions?

Their version of accountability is measured in outcomes, not intentions. They want clarity, transparency, and systems that prove the team is on course.

Here's how to show it:

- Align updates with company priorities. Don't just share activity; share progress tied to strategy.
- Report results with transparency. Include the wins, yes, but also highlight the challenges and what you're doing to address them.
- Keep the communication regular. Don't wait for quarterly reviews; small, consistent updates build more trust than flashy one-off presentations.

Here's the mistake too many leaders make: sugarcoating the story. Sharing only the good news creates a false sense of progress. In contrast, when you admit setbacks and show the plan to overcome them, you demonstrate *real accountability*. Senior leaders don't just want to know you're succeeding; they want to know you're managing reality.

4. Accountability Across Other Departments

No team operates in a bubble. Every decision, handoff, or delay ripples into another department. Accountability, therefore, isn't just vertical (between leaders and their teams)—it's horizontal, stretching across functions.

Ask yourself:

- Are cross-functional teams aligned on what "success" looks like?
- Do other departments really understand your team's role and accountability framework?
- Are there shared processes that keep everyone honest and connected?

Think about marketing. Their accountability isn't just to campaign metrics—it's to the brand's reputation in the public eye. Or finance: they aren't only accountable for closing the books; they're accountable to regulators, investors, and every employee who relies on accurate reporting.

Mapping these relationships across departments shines a light on where collaboration works—and where accountability gets lost in the shuffle.

5. Mapping Stakeholder Conflicts and Synergies

Once you've gathered insights from different stakeholders, the real work begins: putting the pieces together. This means identifying the overlaps but also spotting the friction points before they cause real damage.

For example:

- Your team's desire for autonomy might clash with senior leadership's need for visibility and control.

- A client's push for speed may bump up against your team's commitment to delivering quality.

Neither side is wrong—but without clarity, both sides lose. Recognizing these conflicts early lets you create proactive solutions that balance competing priorities.

A simple tool for this is stakeholder mapping. By visually laying out influence, interests, and expectations, you'll quickly see where accountability lines up and where it doesn't. This makes it easier to prioritize engagement and prevent misalignment before it spreads.

6. Establishing Ongoing Stakeholder Engagement

Accountability isn't "set it and forget it." Stakeholder expectations evolve—new leadership, shifting market conditions, or changing priorities can flip the script overnight. The only way to keep accountability alive is to keep the dialogue open.

Here's how:

- Schedule regular stakeholder check-ins (not just when there's a crisis).

- Build feedback loops through surveys, open forums, or quick touchpoints.
- Update your accountability framework as needs shift.

Case Study: Salesforce – Building Trust Through Transparency

Salesforce sets a gold standard for stakeholder accountability. Through quarterly transparency reports, customer forums, and continuous employee feedback, they keep every group aligned—from leadership to clients to frontline teams. This kind of proactive engagement turns accountability into a shared promise rather than a checklist.

Accountability as a Shared Responsibility

At its core, accountability is never just an internal system—it's a collective commitment. When all stakeholders are engaged, accountability stops feeling like enforcement and starts feeling like ownership.

- Listening to every voice builds stronger buy-in.
- Addressing concerns before they fester prevents friction.
- Integrating diverse perspectives creates a culture where accountability is embraced at every level.

A truly accountable culture doesn't silence differences. It uses them to build alignment, trust, and performance that lasts. At its core, accountability is never just an internal system; it's a collective commitment. When all stakeholders are engaged, accountability stops feeling like enforcement and starts feeling like ownership.

- Listening to every voice builds stronger buy-in.
- Addressing concerns before they fester prevents friction.
- Integrating diverse perspectives creates a culture where accountability is embraced at every level.

Chapter 6: The Nine Steps of Accountability

One of the most effective ways to strengthen accountability within your team is to learn from high-performing teams and organizations. These teams have mastered the balance between ownership, responsibility, and results, making them excellent examples of what works. However, this isn't about blindly copying another company's approach. Instead, it's about extracting positive key principles, understanding why they work, and tailoring them to fit your unique team and organizational culture. By studying the best, you can accelerate progress, avoid common pitfalls, and create a sustainable system of accountability that drives both individual and team success.

The Core Elements of Accountability in High-Performing Teams

When we analyze teams that consistently deliver results, meet deadlines, and drive innovation, common themes emerge. Their success is not by chance—it's built on deliberate strategies and cultural norms that reinforce accountability at every level.

At the heart of every high-performing team lies a structured approach to accountability. This chapter introduces the Nine Step Positive Accountability Wheel, a framework designed to transform accountability from an abstract concept into a clear, actionable system. Each of these steps is a fundamental component of building a culture of ownership, trust, and responsibility. I have been teaching these to leaders in workshops and coaching for over seven years now. They were first introduced to me by a regional director that I worked with in my time leading a retailer. The goal was to create a common language and methodology so that the store teams could improve their accountability skills. At the time there was a lack of consistency and follow-up when it came to managing performance.

We needed to find a better way to ensure that we were building best practices into our leaders and provide them with the skills that would aid them on this quest. Most people have a hard time holding their teams accountable because they don't know how to do it or they are conflict averse. And the problem with accountability without a clear framework is that people shy away from accountability because they assume it will create conflict. However, it is a missing skill that once you learn will transform your leadership forever. And it will change your approach to accountability.

Are you ready to learn what the nine steps of accountability are? Let's dive into each one in detail.

The Nine Steps to Accountability

Step 1: Right Person, Right Role

When it comes to building a successful team, the first step is to make sure you have the right people in the right roles. This means taking the time to assess each employee's skills and strengths and placing them in positions where they can thrive.

It's important to regularly review your team's composition and individual performance to ensure that everyone is in the best position to contribute to the team's overall success. By doing this, you can make any necessary adjustments to optimize your team's performance.

One of the best practices for ensuring the right people are in the right roles is to move beyond traditional annual performance reviews. Instead, today's most effective leaders embrace **continuous performance conversations.** These are short, frequent check-ins that focus on growth, clarity, and accountability. With AI enabled tools, leaders can now track progress in real time, identify skill gaps, and deliver personalized coaching exactly when it's needed.

This approach not only provides timely support and development but also recognizes strengths and accomplishments as they happen. By integrating technology with human insight, businesses create a more dynamic, responsive, and positive culture where performance is not managed once a year but nurtured every day.

From Annual Reviews to Continuous Growth

Old Way: Traditional Performance Reviews	New Way: Innovative, AI-Powered Performance Growth
Annual or semi-annual reviews	Ongoing, real-time feedback and coaching
Focused on past performance	Focused on present growth and future potential
One-size-fits-all evaluation	Personalized insights and development paths
Paperwork-heavy, time-consuming	AI-supported, streamlined, and data-driven
Recognition delayed until review cycle	Recognition and reinforcement in the moment
Often feels judgmental and stagnant	Encourages accountability, learning, and adaptability
Limited manager perspective	Multiple data points—self, peer, customer, and AI analysis
Can disengage or demotivate employees	Builds trust, motivation, and a positive culture

By providing your team with the necessary support and resources, you can help them reach their full potential and contribute to the overall success of your team. In addition to regularly reviewing your team's composition and individual performance, it's also important to stay open to making necessary adjustments.

I can clearly remember a time when I held onto the wrong person for longer than I should have. This impacted the team and the business. Once I made the decision to make the change and part ways with this manager, the team started to thrive. If you lead a team of leaders, one of the most important decisions you make is who you hire and who you promote. Both of these are essential. Assuming you have the right people in the right place, your team will grow and change, and so will their skills and strengths. By being flexible and adaptable, you can ensure that your team is always in the best position to succeed.

Remember, building a successful team is an ongoing process, and it's important to continuously evaluate and make adjustments as needed to keep your team on track. People promote their best sales people to managers which is not always the right thing to do. Assessing if the person's will or skill matches the role and job responsibilities is going to be one of your strengths as a leader. Along with assessing their ability to learn and develop. Like I said earlier in the book, learning agility is a competency that Apple prioritizes, you should know exactly what you are searching for. This will ensure you have the right people in the right place. The questions below can help you reflect on this.

Questions to Ask Yourself:

- Have I accurately assessed the strengths and skills of each team member?
- Are team members in roles that align with their strengths and career goals?
- Have I provided opportunities for employees to use and develop their skills effectively?

Step 2: Expectations Are Clear & Confirmed

A clear understanding of expectations is crucial in any relationship, whether personal or professional. It helps establish a mutual understanding of what is expected from each party and lays a foundation for success.

When setting expectations, it's no longer just about ticking off SMART goals. Today's workforce values **clarity, flexibility, and purpose.** Goals should still be specific and measurable, but they must also adapt to shifting priorities, encourage collaboration, and connect to a bigger "why."

Instead of only asking, "Is *this attainable and time-bound?*" leaders should also ask:

- *"Does this goal inspire growth and innovation?"*
- *"Is it aligned with our team's purpose and values?"*
- *"Can we track progress in real time with the tools we have?"*

By combining clear outcomes with agility, ongoing feedback, and technology (including AI-driven dashboards), leaders create expectations that feel relevant, motivating, and achievable in a fast changing workplace. This approach shifts the focus from simply completing tasks to **driving impact and continuous improvement.**

Communication is another key factor in establishing clear expectations. It is important to communicate expectations clearly and effectively, using language that is easily understood and leaving no room for misinterpretation. To ensure that the message has been received and understood, active listening and feedback are essential. This allows for any misunderstandings to be addressed and resolved before they turn into bigger issues. One thing I truly appreciate about my platform, Ask April AI, is that she helps me formulate my thoughts so that I can clearly articulate what I am trying to say. Did you know that one of the top requests today from humans to Chat GPT is tell me how to say this or tell me how to do this or tell me how to take this idea and put it into a clear road map. Imagine a time when everyone is using AI to clearly define the parameters and communicate them, if the current trend is relevant then isn't it funny to think that chat GPT is actually training us to get clear. That's a thought.

Having a clear understanding of expectations also helps create a more positive and productive work environment. It sets a standard of accountability and responsibility, leading to better performance and outcomes. When expectations are communicated effectively, it promotes transparency and trust between individuals, which is crucial for any successful relationship. Did you know this is the most missed step? Most leaders focus on being clear, telling their teams what they want and walking away without clarifying if their teams understood what was expected. The most important word in this step is *understanding*.

How to Ensure They Really Understand

To ensure someone understands, you must **ask them** to repeat back what they heard you say. After training this to thousands of leaders and helping teams get into alignment, I'm often asked: *"Isn't asking someone to repeat back instructions the same as micromanaging? Isn't that treating my team like children?"*

The answer is **NO**. In fact, micromanaging usually happens when leaders skip this step. Checking for understanding upfront isn't control; it's clarity. It gives you a mirror to your own communication and helps you catch gaps before they turn into bigger problems.

One of the best tips I ever learned even in marriage counseling was to say: *"This is what I heard, is this what you meant?"* Why is this powerful? Because people don't always hear what you said; they hear what they *think* you meant. Without validation, your message can get lost in translation.

And here's the truth about the modern workplace:

- Hybrid and remote teams depend on Zoom, Slack, and project boards. Messages can easily get buried.
- Gen Z and younger employees often crave context and purpose behind the task.
- Seasoned employees value autonomy but still want clear guardrails.

That's why I recommend a simple, supportive script:

> *"To make sure you're set up for success, can you share back what you heard me say so I can validate we're aligned?"*

Notice the tone. It's not about testing them, it's about making sure they're fully equipped to succeed. It also signals psychological safety: you're giving them permission to admit if something wasn't clear.

Example in Action: Imagine you're leading a hybrid team and you delegate: *"Can you prepare the sales deck for Friday's client meeting?"* Your team member nods, but what did they actually hear?

- Did they think you meant a full presentation or just a few updated slides?
- Did they understand the deadline was *end of day Thursday* so you could review it?
- Did they know the deck needed to match the new brand template?

Without checking, you may find yourself frustrated on Friday when the deck isn't what you expected. But if you asked them to recap, you might hear:

> *"Sure, so you'd like me to have the updated deck with the new branding ready by Thursday EOD so you can review before Friday's client meeting, correct?"*

You would have instantly confirmed alignment. That's accountability in action.

Modern Leader Tip: Setting Expectations That Stick

- **Use Multiple Channels**
  Don't rely on one conversation follow up with a quick Slack, email, or task assignment.

- **Leverage Technology**

  Use tools like Asana, Trello, or Notion so goals are visible and trackable.

- **Create Psychological Safety**

  Frame your ask as clarity, not a test: "*I want to make sure I was clear.*"

- **Adapt to Generational Styles**

  Gen Z often values context and purpose; seasoned employees value autonomy.

- **Normalize "Repeat Back"**

  Make it part of your culture. Over time, your team will do it automatically.

The modern workforce doesn't need more control; it needs more clarity. It needs more agency and more understanding.

Questions to Ask Yourself:

- Have I clearly communicated the expectations and goals to my team?

- Do team members understand their individual responsibilities and how they contribute to the overall goals? How do I know?

- Have I verified my team has a full understanding by asking for feedback or clarification from team members? ASK "what is your understanding of the expected outcome we are trying to reach?

- Or What is your understanding of what I'm asking of you?" "Walk me through what you heard me say?"

Step 3: Agreed Consequences for Missed Expectations

If expectations are not met, it is important to agree on consequences that are fair and well-known between all parties involved. This ensures that everyone is on the same page and understands the potential outcomes if expectations are not met. These consequences should also be discussed and documented to avoid any confusion or misunderstandings in the future.

One of the best practices for this step is to make sure that the consequences are consistent. This means that they should be the same for all parties involved, regardless of their role or position. This helps to avoid any feelings of unfairness or favoritism. Additionally, the consequences should be known to all parties involved to create a sense of accountability and responsibility. This can also serve as a deterrent for not meeting expectations.

In addition to being fair and consistent, consequences should also be discussed and agreed upon beforehand. This allows all parties to have a say in the consequences and ensures that they are reasonable and appropriate for the situation. By documenting these consequences, there is also a clear record of what was agreed upon and can be referred back to if needed. I remember clearly when this happened to me twice.

Once my manager told me, "Hey April, if you don't get this task done, when it comes to be promoted, I won't be recommending you." It might sound harsh but I appreciated that she clarified what the expectations were. In essence, she said to me "Because you are choosing not to be compliant in this area, it won't merit a promotion."

Do you notice the language here? You are choosing, because you validated that you understand this is an expectation. Another thing she always did when coaching was ask, "Hey, I'd like to give you some feedback, but before I do, can you tell me what the expectations are as it pertains to ...(fill in the gap)?" If I shared the expectation correctly, she would then ask me what was causing me to decide not to meet them? Instead of doing what most leaders do who would give me feedback and ask me to change it next time, she had me tell her what I understood and then asked me why I was choosing if I knew not to comply.

Do you see the difference?

She would also tell me in advance that if I kept making that choice, I was accepting the consequences. I learned a lot from her. She was a fair leader, excellent coach and ran a tight ship. I took ownership and stepped up and decided to make the change. So many leaders are afraid of having that conversation, but it shaped my career. I made the change, and when the time came to be promoted, I was. Imagine if she had not told me the consequences of my inaction?

This step helps to create a sense of trust and transparency between all parties involved and can lead to better communication, ownership and problem-solving in the future.

In workshops we practice this and teach it, and it is always mind-blowing when the lights in leaders' brains switch on and they realize they do all the talking instead of switching to asking questions. This is why we teach coaching skills and the art of asking questions.

Questions to Ask Yourself:

- Have I discussed and agreed upon the consequences of not meeting expectations with my team?
- Are the consequences fair, consistent, and known to all team members?
- Have I documented the agreed-upon consequences and shared them with the team?

Step 4: Create a Detailed Follow-Up Plan

After creating a follow-up plan, it is important to establish a timeline for reviewing progress. This can be done by setting up checkpoints and using tools such as calendars and reminders to stay organized and on track. By incorporating time management practices, like scheduling follow-up tasks in your calendar, you can ensure that you are consistently making progress toward your goals.

Creating a follow-up schedule allows you to break down the larger plan into smaller, achievable tasks. By setting specific dates and deadlines, you can hold yourself accountable and stay motivated to complete each step. This also allows you to track progress and make necessary adjustments to your plan along the way.

I know lots of leaders complain about not having enough time but in reality, planning your follow up and making sure the details are planned out will ensure you don't miss a deadline. And you will be using your time wisely. OKR's are helpful for small and large businesses, however without dates and checkpoints in place it will be hard to hold yourself and the team accountable. A good way to transfer ownership is to ask your team to send you a follow up and get them and then to send you an invite for the follow up. This stops you from having to constantly follow up. I find it helpful to put due dates in my calendar before the actual due date.

Questions to Ask Yourself:

- Have I created a follow-up plan with specific checkpoints to review progress?
- Am I using tools like calendars and reminders to stay on track?
- Do I regularly check in with team members to review progress and provide support?

Best Practice Tip: Implement "Friday Follow-Up" go through past requests and follow up on outstanding items.

Step 5: Course Correct as Needed

After setting a specific goal and following through with the necessary steps, it is important to regularly check in and assess progress. This could include receiving feedback from others, evaluating personal performance, or re-evaluating the initial goal itself. By being flexible and open to making adjustments, one can ensure that the desired outcome is achieved in the most effective and efficient way possible.

Best practices for this stage include encouraging a positive culture of continuous improvement. This means fostering an environment where mistakes are seen as opportunities for growth and feedback is welcomed. It also involves being receptive to suggestions and open to trying new approaches.

By creating a supportive and encouraging atmosphere, individuals are more likely to feel motivated and empowered to make the necessary adjustments for success. A best practice here is to have your team check in with you along the process. When you do this you avoid projects going off track. Coaching is important in this step. Asking questions, providing honest fact based feedback that is based on where you are to the expected outcomes and project timelines.

Questions to Ask Yourself:

- Am I flexible and open to adjusting based on team progress and feedback?
- Am I assessing the impact on the business?
- Do I encourage a positive culture of continuous improvement and learning?
- What can I do to help my team grow?
- How can I support them in achieving the goal?

Leadership Reminder: Ownership belongs to the team—let your managers know they should come to you if they get stuck.

Step 6: Be Consistent, Be Involved

Consistency and involvement are crucial for reinforcing accountability and trust within a team. A leader who consistently checks in, supports, and engages with their team creates an environment where accountability is embedded in everyday interactions rather than something enforced sporadically. When leaders maintain regular follow-ups and demonstrate reliability in their actions, it fosters a culture where employees feel valued and supported.

Being consistent doesn't mean micromanaging but rather ensuring that your presence is felt in a way that encourages growth and development. Employees thrive when they know their leader is available, approachable, and invested in their success. This means holding regular one-on-one meetings, staying engaged in team discussions, and following through on commitments.

I had a founder once ask me, isn't this called micromanaging? There are so many myths around micromanaging: what it is and what it is not. Being involved means that you are checking in, you know what's going on and you have a clear path and line of communication with your team to ensure you get what you need. In a hierarchy of large organizations, this is very important. When you insert yourself in the process to check in, do not take over. Go in with an open mind, lowering resistance by asking a ton of questions. Your job is to stay involved but not take over. Remember this.

Consistency also applies to the expectations and consequences set forth in previous steps. If a leader inconsistently applies accountability measures letting some missed deadlines slide while strictly enforcing others it creates confusion and a lack of motivation within the team. Trust erodes when employees perceive favoritism or unpredictability in their leader's actions. Instead, maintaining fairness, transparency, and structured follow-ups ensures a stable and high-performing team.

It is also essential to strike a balance between focusing on low performers and recognizing top achievers. Too often, leaders spend the bulk of their time trying to "fix" employees who struggle while neglecting those who consistently excel. The best approach is to provide a structured system where all employees whether struggling or excelling receive the necessary attention and resources.

Being involved means actively supporting your team's growth. Are you regularly checking in on development plans? Are you helping individuals identify their strengths and areas of improvement? Do your team members know they can count on you for guidance?

A simple yet effective way to build involvement is through regularly scheduled follow-ups and strategic engagement with employees. Whether through daily check-ins, weekly development meetings, or monthly performance reviews, your involvement should be steady and meaningful.

Questions to ask yourself:

- Am I consistently involved in my team's progress and development?
- Do I maintain regular check-ins and provide ongoing support to my team?

- Are my check-ins structured and meaningful, or are they ad-hoc and inconsistent?
- Do I focus too much on low performers while neglecting high achievers?
- Have I built trust with my team by being reliable and consistent in my actions?
- Where am I falling short in demonstrating my involvement?

Step 7: Assume Nothing

One of the biggest obstacles to accountability is the tendency to make assumptions. Leaders often assume that their team members understand expectations, know what success looks like, or are aware of impending consequences. Unfortunately, assumptions can lead to misunderstandings, missed opportunities, and disengagement. We assume a lot. I ask leaders all the time, is that a fact or an assumption? Many times the stories we make up in our heads are just that-a story and not grounded in real facts. Again, asking questions is a skill and it's one that is underdeveloped in many leaders. However, jumping to conclusions is one that they know very well.

A leader must always verify rather than assume. This means asking clarifying questions, ensuring all expectations are communicated clearly, and fostering a culture of open dialogue. Miscommunication is one of the primary reasons for failed accountability when employees don't fully understand their responsibilities, it's impossible for them to meet expectations.

Creating a culture of open and honest conversations helps eliminate assumptions. Employees should feel comfortable asking for clarity and guidance without fear of judgment. This is particularly important in teams with diverse work styles, experience levels, or cultural backgrounds. A leader who assumes that all employees operate the same way will quickly encounter resistance and confusion.

Instead of assuming, actively engage with your team. Ask questions that confirm understanding, encourage feedback, and create opportunities for team members to voice concerns. Regular team meetings, one-on-one check-ins, and structured feedback loops help leaders stay connected and informed about team dynamics.

Additionally, leaders should avoid making assumptions about why an employee may not be performing well. Instead of assuming lack of effort or commitment, take the time to explore external factors such as workload challenges, unclear expectations, or personal difficulties that may be impacting performance. If you are going to make an assumption, assume positive intent.

I remember having this conversation once with my team. I was hosting a leadership offsite and one of the leaders asked me how they could assume positive intent. It's easy, always assume everyone is doing their best until they prove you otherwise. It puts you in a positive open curious mindset. When you approach team members with this mindset you will open up conversations otherwise not available to you. I learned to assume positive intent when I worked at Apple. This was a big part of the company's culture. And I truly believe that if more leaders would do this, positivity would spread. You see most of us are hard wired to think negatively and always go to the worst case scenario. Don't get stuck discussing and speculating what you believe is true. This is wasted time and energy that could be spent on following up, problem solving or new ideas.

Stop Assuming, Start Asking

One of the biggest dangers to accountability is assumption. When performance slips, many leaders default to negative assumptions:

- "They don't care."
- "They're lazy."
- "They're not committed."

But rarely is that the full truth. More often, the real issues are unclear expectations, workload challenges, or personal factors that haven't surfaced.

Here's the shift: if you're going to make an assumption, **assume positive intent**. Approach every situation believing your team is doing their best until proven otherwise. This mindset puts you in a space of curiosity instead of judgment. It invites dialogue instead of shutting it down.

I remember a leader at one of my offsites asking, "*But how do you assume positive intent when you're not sure?*" My answer: it's simple. Start with the belief that your team is showing up to succeed, not to fail. At Apple, this was part of the culture, and it transformed how leaders built trust.

Why does this matter? Because negative assumptions erode accountability. When leaders speculate or gossip about why someone isn't performing, they waste energy and create a culture of blame. When leaders assume positive intent, they create space for follow-up, problem-solving, and new ideas.

Accountability thrives when clarity replaces assumption. If you catch yourself speculating, stop and ask.

Negative Assumptions	Positive Intent
"They don't care about this project."	"Maybe the goal or deadline wasn't clear. Let me check in."
"They're not committed."	"They're probably balancing multiple priorities. How can I help clarify what's most important?"
"They're lazy."	"Maybe they don't have the tools or training yet. What support do they need?"
"They just don't get it."	"Did I test for understanding? Let me ask them to recap what they heard."
"They're making excuses."	"What obstacles are in the way? How can we problem-solve together?"

When you assume negative intent, you close down conversations and accountability weakens. When you assume positive intent, you open conversations and strengthen accountability.

Questions to ask yourself:

- Am I making assumptions about my team members' performance or understanding?
- Do I actively seek clarification and encourage open dialogue with my team?
- Have I provided opportunities for team members to voice their concerns and ask questions?
- Am I aware of individual working styles, challenges, and motivations within my team?
- Am I asking questions with a curious mindset?
- How do I ensure clarity in expectations and communication?

Leader's Reflection: Reframing Assumptions

Think of a recent situation where someone on your team didn't meet your expectations.

1. **Write down your first assumption.**
   What was the story you told yourself about why it happened?

2. **Check the evidence.**
   Was this assumption based on facts, or on what you *believed* to be true?

3. **Reframe with positive intent.**
   How could you reframe the story by assuming they were doing their best?

4. **Plan your follow-up.**
   What's one clarifying question you can ask that opens dialogue instead of closing it?

Example:

Assumption: *"They missed the deadline because they don't care."*

Reframe: *"They may not have understood the priority or timeline. Let me ask what got in the way."*

Clarifying Question: *"Can you walk me through what impacted the timing so we can figure out how to prevent it next time?"*

Practicing this exercise regularly rewires your leadership reflex from judgment to curiosity, the foundation of positive accountability.

Step 8: Recognize Performance

Recognition is a powerful driver of accountability. Employees who feel seen, valued, and appreciated for their hard work are more likely to maintain high levels of commitment and responsibility. When leaders acknowledge achievements, both big and small, they reinforce the behaviors they want to see repeated.

A culture of recognition doesn't just focus on the highest achievers; it should include every team member who contributes meaningfully to the organization's success. Publicly acknowledging wins in meetings, sending personal thank-you messages, or celebrating milestones through formal recognition programs all play a role in sustaining engagement. Recognizing performance also includes providing specific and timely feedback. Saying, "Great job" is nice, but saying, "You did a great job managing that difficult client situation and keeping the project on track under pressure" is much more meaningful. Specific feedback helps employees understand exactly what they did well and encourages them to replicate that behavior in the future.

It's also important to create structured recognition systems that ensure consistency. Some teams implement a "Friday Follow-Up" where leaders take time at the end of the week to send out messages of appreciation. Every Friday, I had planned into my calendar to mail out two to five appreciation cards. This was to ensure I looked for something or someone to celebrate weekly. Even now with a small team, I try to recognize effort, output, and ideas. It is very important to be a great boss and make sure people feel valued.

Others establish peer recognition programs where employees can nominate colleagues for their contributions.

Leaders should also be mindful of balancing positive reinforcement with constructive feedback. While it's essential to celebrate wins, it's equally important to ensure employees are growing and developing.

Questions to ask yourself:

- Am I regularly acknowledging and celebrating my team's achievements?
- Do I provide timely and specific positive feedback to reinforce desired behaviors?
- Have I created a culture of recognition and appreciation within my team?
- Do I have structured systems for recognizing performance, or is it inconsistent?
- Am I ensuring that all team members, not just the top performers, receive recognition?

Step 9: If the Outcome is Not Successful, Refer to Step 1

Accountability is an ongoing process. If performance issues persist, or if goals are not met, it's crucial to revisit the fundamentals rather than placing blame. This means going back to Step 1 and reassessing whether the right people are in the right roles, whether expectations are clear, and whether the support systems in place are adequate.

Revisiting the process allows leaders to identify gaps and make necessary adjustments. Perhaps an employee needs additional training, clearer guidance, or a different approach to motivation. Perhaps the structure of the team needs to be re-evaluated, or new strategies need to be implemented to enhance performance.

If repeated attempts to improve performance fail, leaders should also consider whether the employee is the right fit for the role. Not every team member will thrive in every position, and sometimes reassignment or career development discussions are necessary to align talent with the right opportunities.

This final step reinforces the idea that accountability isn't about punishment; it's about continuous improvement. Leaders who adopt a growth mindset and encourage their teams to learn from setbacks will build stronger, more resilient organizations. Sometimes you may have to make the decision to end a working relationship with someone on your team and promote them to customers. This happens when you've followed every step with your team. And if you do, I can almost guarantee that the person you are holding accountable will quit if they are not performing prior to you having to fire them. However, if you do have to terminate someone, make sure it is not a surprise because you've followed every step.

Questions to ask yourself:

- If goals are not met, have I revisited the process to identify gaps or issues?
- Have I reassessed roles, expectations, and support structures to implement necessary changes?
- Do I encourage my team to view setbacks as opportunities for learning and growth?
- Am I open to adjusting strategies and providing additional resources as needed?
- Have I explored all possible solutions before making personnel changes?

- Do I need to promote this team member to customer? In other words, terminate their employment.

I am including a checklist that you can use and download at aprilsabral.com.

Here's a checklist based on the Nine Steps of Accountability Framework that aligns with my leadership philosophy and practical approach to fostering accountability:.

Accountability Checklist: Nine Steps for Leaders

Right People, Right Place

- Have I assessed each team member's strengths and skills?
- Are team members in roles that align with their abilities and career goals?
- Have I made necessary adjustments to optimize team performance?

Clear Understanding of Expectations

- Have I communicated expectations clearly and effectively?
- Did I validate understanding by asking team members to recap or confirm?
- Are expectations specific, measurable, and tied to outcomes?

Agree on Mutual Consequences

- Have I discussed and agreed upon the consequences for unmet expectations? Is my team clear?
- Are the consequences fair, consistent, and documented?

- Do team members understand the impact of their choices?

Create a Detailed Follow-Up Plan

- Have I set specific checkpoints to review progress?
- Am I using tools like calendars or reminders to stay organized?
- Have I delegated follow-up ownership to team members where appropriate?

Course Correct as Needed

- Am I regularly assessing progress and providing feedback?
- Do I encourage a culture of continuous improvement and learning?
- Have I identified and addressed obstacles proactively?

Be Consistent, Be Involved

- Am I consistently engaged with my team's progress?
- Do I balance attention between high performers and those needing support?
- Have I built trust through reliability and structured follow-ups?

Assume Nothing

- Have I verified understanding rather than making assumptions?
- Am I asking clarifying questions to ensure alignment?
- Do I approach team members with a mindset of positive intent?

Recognize Performance

- Am I regularly acknowledging and celebrating achievements?
- Is my feedback specific, timely, and meaningful?
- Have I created structured systems for recognition?

If the Outcome is Not Successful, Refer to Step 1

- Have I revisited the fundamentals to identify gaps?

- Am I open to adjusting roles, expectations, or strategies?
- Have I exhausted all efforts before considering personnel changes?

This checklist is designed to guide leaders in embedding accountability into their daily practices while fostering trust, clarity, and growth.

The Positive Accountability Wheel.

Diagram Taken from The Positive Effect Leadership System &
Workshop

By incorporating these nine steps into leadership practices, teams can cultivate a culture of accountability that is both fair and effective. Each step builds upon the last, creating a structured approach to leadership that emphasizes clarity, consistency, and continuous improvement. High-performing teams are not built overnight, but through intentional and thoughtful leadership, organizations can foster an environment where accountability thrives, and results follow.

Case Studies: How Leading Companies Drive Accountability

Many successful companies have built cultures of accountability that reinforce trust, ownership, and high performance.

Google's Project Oxygen found that the best managers create a system of regular feedback and structured check-ins, keeping accountability at the forefront. Similarly, Toyota's Lean Management System relies on continuous improvement (Kaizen) and root-cause analysis to eliminate assumptions and enhance accountability.

Apple's leadership approach is rooted in attention to detail and active involvement. Leaders stay engaged in projects from concept to execution, ensuring team members are held accountable while feeling supported. Meanwhile, Netflix employs a "Keeper Test" approach, where leaders regularly evaluate if employees are in the right roles and provide direct, transparent feedback. When team members do not meet expectations, Netflix proactively reassesses fit instead of allowing mediocrity to persist.

These case studies reinforce that accountability is not about micromanagement; it's about creating systems that support autonomy, clarity, and performance.

Applying the Nine Steps to Build a Culture of Accountability

By implementing the Nine Steps, teams can:

✓ Foster ownership over tasks and responsibilities.

✓ Build trust and transparency across the organization.

✓ Improve performance and collaboration.

Call to Action: Select one area from the Nine Steps and apply it to your team this week. Small shifts lead to big transformations! Take the Accountability Index Assessment and get your personal development plan on how you can improve your positive accountability. Even better, have your team complete the assessment and then discuss your results.

Chapter 7: Engaging Team Members in the Accountability Process

One of the biggest challenges organizations face is shifting to a culture of accountability especially when leadership changes or a new team steps in with a different approach. This shift can create uncertainty, resistance, or even disengagement among team members. However, fostering true accountability is not about imposing top-down directives; rather, it requires collaboration, transparency, and shared ownership.

I can remember taking over teams where accountability was not embraced. When this happened, I would paint a vision of the future and then get them engaged in a meaningful way. I would share stories of how in the past I'd experienced poor leadership, what I learned from it, and then how I grew in those moments along with personal stories of success. After leading teams and training over thousands of leaders from stages and workshops, I can tell you that story telling goes a long way in gaining buy-in. Sharing stories of success and failures. This shows your track record, makes you human and helps the team come along on a journey with you.

When I was at DAVIDsTEA, I created a notebook for each of my team. I had taken over a team of thirty-five multi-site leaders. I knew they were going to be skeptical of my leadership. After all, who was I? So I put a plan together to gain trust buy-in immediately so that I could start to gain traction with my team. The notebook was a gift that set a standard. Inside the notepad it read: fill this notepad with meaningful moments. It was a really great way to set a tone.

Setting new standards and expectations can be difficult for people, when they have been doing things a certain way for so long. Change causes resistance. In the positive effect workshops we teach the six supporting blocks of change. I mentioned these earlier in the book. The first block that moves people towards change is vision. Vision is as simple as sharing what your vision is with your team. Making sure it has substance and a clear path forwards. When setting vision around improving accountability it could sound like this. Our vision as a team is to improve performance and productivity by ensuring our team is trained on a nine step accountability framework. This will enable us to develop our talent and people. With a heightened focus on improving the step of accountability we operate under, we will see much better team engagement which in turn will result in higher sales. Our vision is for all leaders to be comfortable holding their team accountable and see it as a positive step in leading their team.

Once, I made a vision board together with my team. I then gifted them a notepad with the text on it that read: This is our make a difference with people notepad. Fill this book with stories about people who make a difference for our customers. This is the journey we are creating together.

Building a sustainable accountability framework means engaging team members at every level. Without their participation and buy-in, even the best laid plans can falter. Resistance whether active or passive can derail progress before it even begins. This is why we spend time talking about the six support blocks and the six pillars that reduce and lower resistance to you as a leader in our training. The key to success lies in fostering understanding, creating alignment, and ensuring that every team member sees the value in the process.

Transparent Communication: Setting the Foundation

Accountability thrives in a culture of transparency. Leaders must go beyond merely explaining why accountability is important; they must demonstrate how it benefits the team and organization. This involves clear and concise communication that resonates with all team members.

Instead of corporate jargon or technical terminology, frame the discussion around shared values and collective benefits, such as:

✓ Improved team performance

✓ Better project outcomes

✓ A more supportive work environment

✓ Increased individual growth opportunities

✓ A stronger sense of collective purpose

Transparency also means creating space for two-way communication. Open dialogue fosters trust, engagement, and a deeper commitment to accountability. Leaders should organize team meetings or workshops dedicated to discussing the accountability process. Encouraging questions, addressing concerns, and actively listening to feedback makes employees feel valued and creates a sense of shared ownership.

By inviting team members to help shape the accountability process, they become co-creators rather than passive recipients of change.

Involving Team Members in the Design Process

People are more likely to embrace change when they have a role in shaping it. Instead of rolling out a rigid accountability structure, involve team members early in the design and implementation process. We highly suggest if you don't have a framework that you adopt the nine steps and then workshop it out as a team as to what it could look like. This is what we do with our clients.

Here's how leaders can increase buy-in and participation:

- Create small working groups – Gather employees from different roles and levels to brainstorm ideas and refine processes.
- Allow feedback on new policies – Before finalizing an accountability framework, ask team members for their insights and concerns.
- Encourage active participation – Turn team members

into accountability champions who help drive engagement among their peers.

When employees have a voice in the process, they feel invested in its success. Instead of resisting accountability, they embrace it as something they helped create. Going back to my retail leadership days, the time I brought in leaders from the field to work with the support and HQ teams was one of the most valuable moments. Even going further back when I was a store manager and I was invited to sit at the table with senior leaders it got me brought into the process of improvement. Most recently, I was reminded that when I don't include my team, they feel confused and skeptical due to vague and non-focused communication.

Maintaining Momentum: Check-Ins & Continuous Feedback

Once the framework is in place, ongoing engagement is crucial. Regular check-ins both formal and informal help maintain momentum and address emerging challenges.

These check-ins should focus on more than just performance metrics.

Leaders should ask:

"Are team members finding the accountability process effective?"

"Are there obstacles preventing full engagement?"

"Do we need to adjust expectations or resources?"

This continuous feedback loop ensures that accountability remains a supportive and evolving process rather than a rigid or punitive system. When I was at Apple, they had a process called fearless feedback. It provided a framework for everyone, regardless of title, to take ownership and responsibility for giving feedback. They took this one step further and trained their employees in onboarding to be a good *getter* of feedback. This was the first time I had experienced this type of rigor and accountability regarding feedback. Imagine everyone on your team being trained on how to receive it (I didn't say agree with it) and provide that feedback to others on the team.

Additionally, transparency in performance reviews reinforces trust. A clear, fair, and structured system helps employees understand how their progress is measured. Feedback should be:

✓ Constructive And Fact Based – Focused on solutions rather than criticism and facts versus opinions.

✓ Specific – Providing clear insights on what's working and what needs improvement.

✓ Timely – Delivered consistently, not just during annual reviews.

By keeping lines of communication open, teams are more likely to remain engaged, motivated, and aligned with organizational goals.

Fostering a Culture of Peer-to-Peer Accountability

True accountability does not come solely from leadership— it flourishes when team members hold each other accountable in a constructive way. Leaders should encourage a culture where employees support and challenge each other in positive, respectful, and collaborative ways.

This can be achieved through:

◆ Regular team meetings – Where progress updates are shared, and challenges are discussed openly.

◆ Peer feedback sessions – Where employees provide constructive, solution-focused feedback to colleagues.

◆ Clear feedback guidelines – Ensuring that accountability discussions remain productive, professional, and free from negativity. Just like Apple with their fearless feedback model.

By shifting the mindset from hierarchical accountability to shared responsibility, teams develop a sense of unity and purpose. When I worked at Apple, they had a clear framework called fearless accountability, this made everyone responsible for shared feedback at all levels.

Recently, I was talking to a president of a company who shared that they have quarterly offsites where they share feedback openly to one another using the precast that is for the best of the individual and the business. So when sharing feedback, having this in mind versus what it made me feel like, makes it less personal and more productive. Focusing on habits, behaviors and patterns also help lower resistance. It could sound like this.

Feedback Statement to a peer, or supervisor.

"When I receive meeting requests or important information last-minute like the email sent twenty minutes before our last meeting it limits my ability to prepare thoroughly. This directly impacts my performance, as I'm not able to contribute at the level I expect of myself. When that happens, it affects the quality of our team discussions and slows down our ability to make aligned decisions efficiently. To prevent this, I need at least 48 hours' notice so I can prepare and bring my best to the table."

Using Technology to Enhance Engagement

Technology can serve as a powerful enabler of accountability by making progress tracking, goal setting, and communication more efficient.

Consider integrating:

✦ Project management software – For clear visibility into tasks, deadlines, and responsibilities. I love Notion, however there are many on the market now.

✦ Collaboration platforms – To foster open communication and real-time feedback. Even a group text is simple but effective.

✦ Surveys & feedback tools – To collect insights and measure employee engagement in the process. I highly recommend you always ask for feedback.

When technology supports accountability, teams are more likely to stay aligned, informed, and engaged.

Addressing Fear of Failure & Psychological Safety

One of the biggest barriers to accountability is fear: fear of judgment, criticism, or making mistakes. If employees believe that taking ownership comes with punishment rather than learning, they will actively avoid accountability.

Leaders must foster psychological safety, where employees feel comfortable taking risks, experimenting, and learning from setbacks. This means:

✓ Encouraging a growth mindset – Mistakes should be seen as learning opportunities, not failures. We call it above and below the line leadership. This simple but effective way of thinking helps leaders identify when they are shifting into negativity and blame.

✓ Leading by example – Leaders should openly share their own challenges and lessons learned. Like I shared earlier, telling stories about when I realized and learned from leaders who used the nine steps shifted my leadership and thinking and then caused me to step up and take ownership. I can't tell you how many times in workshops, as soon as I share a personal story the frameworks we are teaching resonates with the participants and they get it. It validates and puts it in context.

✓ Valuing development over blame – Shift from "Who is responsible for this mistake?" to "How can we improve?"

When employees see accountability as a pathway to growth rather than punishment, they lean into responsibility rather than avoiding it.

Recognizing and Rewarding Accountability

People are more likely to embrace accountability when they see that it leads to positive outcomes.

Leaders should:

- Publicly recognize team accomplishments – Celebrate wins in meetings or newsletters.
- Acknowledge effort and progress – Send personal messages or shoutouts.

- Offer incentives and career opportunities – Show that accountability leads to growth, promotions, or rewards.

Positive reinforcement creates a cycle of motivation and engagement—where accountability is not seen as a burden, but a source of pride and accomplishment.

Building a culture of accountability is not a one-time event— it is a continuous process that requires commitment, flexibility, and open collaboration.

By focusing on:

- Transparent communication
- Involving employees in the process
- Continuous feedback and adaptation
- Psychological safety & a growth mindset
- Recognizing and rewarding accountability

Most importantly: Implementing a proven framework like the nine steps of accountability

Leaders turn accountability from a task into a mindset. When team members feel engaged and empowered, accountability becomes a natural and valued part of the culture not something imposed from above.

With the right approach, accountability ceases to be a challenge and becomes the driving force behind a high-performing, resilient, and motivated team.

Chapter 8: The Mirror of Leadership Self-Reflection and Accountability

Leadership is often viewed as the ability to guide, inspire, and hold others accountable. However, true accountability begins within. The most effective leaders are those who regularly self-reflect, evaluate their own behaviors, and take responsibility for their actions before expecting the same from their teams. This chapter explores how self-reflection plays a crucial role in developing positive, accountable leadership and provides practical exercises for leaders to enhance their self-awareness and growth.

The Power of Self-Reflection in Leadership

Self-reflection is the process of looking inward to examine one's thoughts, emotions, and actions. It allows leaders to pause, assess their decisions, and ensure alignment with their values and leadership goals. Without self-reflection, it is easy to fall into patterns of reactive leadership, making decisions without understanding their long-term impact.

A positive, accountable leader does not merely delegate responsibility; they model it. Leaders ask me all the time, "How do I get my team to take on more and own their roles? I say, "Lead by example." When you are conscious of your influence and ensure your leadership is a mirror reflecting accountability, integrity, and consistency, your team's accountability will improve.

Self-reflection strengthens a leader's ability to:

- Identify strengths and areas for improvement.

- Recognize biases and blind spots.

- Align daily actions with long-term goals.

- Improve communication and decision-making.

- Foster a culture of trust and accountability within their team.

Self-Assessment: How Accountable Are You?

Before leaders can cultivate accountability in their teams, they must first evaluate their own accountability practices. The following self-assessment questions will help you gauge your level of accountability and identify areas for growth:

- Do I take full ownership of my decisions, or do I sometimes shift blame?

- When things go wrong, do I seek solutions or make excuses?
- How often do I reflect on my leadership style and its impact on my team?
- Do I follow through on commitments, or do I find myself making exceptions?
- How comfortable am I with receiving and acting on constructive feedback?
- Do I communicate expectations clearly, and do I hold myself to the same standard I expect from my team?

Reflecting on these questions can highlight patterns in your leadership behavior. Identifying areas where accountability may be lacking is the first step in making meaningful changes.

Cultivating a Habit of Self-Reflection

Developing a habit of self-reflection requires intention and consistency. Here are some strategies to help integrate self-reflection into your leadership practice:

1. Daily Reflection Time

Set aside 10-15 minutes each day to review your actions, decisions, and interactions. Journaling can be an effective way to document your thoughts and track your progress over time.

2. Seek Honest Feedback

Encourage open and honest feedback from peers, mentors, and team members. A culture of accountability starts when leaders demonstrate they are willing to listen, learn, and improve.

3. Practice the 3 R's: Recognize, Reframe, and Respond

Recognize moments where accountability could have been stronger. Reframe your perspective by asking, "What could I have done differently?" Respond by implementing small changes to improve future outcomes.

4. Ask Yourself Tough Questions

Great leaders challenge themselves with difficult questions that encourage deep self-exploration, such as:

- What example am I setting for my team?

- How do I react when faced with challenges?
- Am I actively developing my leadership skills, or am I relying on past experiences?
- If I had to rate myself today on my performance like I rate my team, where would I rank?

The Role of Mindset in Accountability

Accountability is not just about actions; it is also about mindset. A leader with a positive growth mindset views challenges as opportunities and setbacks as learning experiences. Shifting from a fixed mindset ("This is just how I lead") to a growth mindset ("I can always improve my leadership skills") can lead to greater self-awareness and stronger leadership accountability. I have worked with leaders who are the role models of both. If you are going to be one, pick the growth mindset. Positive Culture is hard to cultivate without it. Actually I'll even go as far as to say it's impossible.

Leaders Who Reflect and Adapt

Consider the story of a retail executive who struggled with employee turnover. At first, she attributed the issue to a weak labor market, but after self-reflection, she realized her leadership style lacked consistent feedback and development opportunities for employees. By making adjustments, implementing structured one-on-one meetings, creating clear career paths, and fostering open dialogue she saw increased employee retention and engagement. This transformation was only possible because she took accountability for her leadership approach. Stop using weather, no good employees and other reasoning for why your business is not thriving. This just sets you up for failure. Take ownership! Review what can be improved and ensure you communicate that with your team using the Nine Step Wheel.

Just recently we were working on a project and one member of my team was excited to share what she had created. When I took a look at it, I realized that it was not aligned with what our client wanted. Instead of getting stressed and blaming her for not listening, I asked myself whether I was really clear and how we could have made sure we were on the same page. People don't want to fail or disappoint; they want to succeed and earn recognition for their work. So, I took responsibility for the miscommunication.

There have been many times in my career where I thought I'd been clear only to find out that, in reality, I was only clear in my mind. I did not communicate with the same level of clarity. I hear so many leaders blame their teams when things go wrong. However, those moments when you missed the mark will determine whether your team grows to respect you or starts looking for another job.

Self-accountability is hard, it requires us to look in the mirror. It also requires us to put time aside for it. And we all know how valuable our time is as leaders and business owners. But there is no greater investment of time than in the team that is the foundation of your business.

Action Steps for Developing Personal Accountability

To solidify the practice of self-reflection and accountability, here are actionable steps you can implement immediately:

1. Create a Leadership Reflection Journal
   - Write down key decisions, challenges, and outcomes.
   - Reflect on what went well and what could be improved.
   - Identify action steps for growth.

2. Set Personal Accountability Goals

- Commit to specific improvements in your leadership approach.
- Set measurable goals such as improving communication, increasing delegation, or enhancing team trust.

3. Schedule Regular Check-ins with Yourself

- Block time on your calendar for self-reflection sessions.
- Use this time to assess progress and make necessary adjustments.

4. Develop an Accountability Partner System

- Partner with another leader or mentor for accountability check-ins.
- Share insights, challenges, and strategies for growth.

Leadership accountability starts with self-awareness. By incorporating regular self-reflection, seeking honest feedback, and making intentional changes, leaders can become powerful examples of accountability in action. The journey to becoming a positive, accountable leader is ongoing, but the more you engage in self-reflection, the stronger your leadership impact will be.

As you move into the next chapter, consider the ripple effect of your accountability. Your leadership behaviors set the tone for your team, and by modeling self-awareness and personal responsibility, you empower others to do the same.

Chapter 9: The Ripple Effect of Accountability – How Your Leadership Shapes Others

Leadership is not just about individual performance; it is about the influence you have on those around you. John C. Maxwell goes as far as to say, "Leadership is Influence, nothing more, nothing less." Every decision, action, and behavior you model sends a message to your team about what is acceptable and what is expected. This chapter explores the long-term impact of accountable leadership on teams, business culture, and individual growth. It will help leaders see how their approach to accountability influences team morale, trust, and overall performance, reinforcing the idea that leadership is about modeling the behaviors you want to see in others.

> Leadership is not just about individual performance; it is about the influence you have on those around you.

The Power of Leading by Example

One of the most effective ways to instill accountability in others is by demonstrating it yourself. When leaders consistently uphold their commitments, take responsibility for their actions, and remain open to feedback, they set a powerful precedent for their teams.

Trust is built through consistency. Employees are more likely to follow through on commitments when they see their leaders doing the same. Performance improves when expectations are clear. Accountable leaders provide clarity and structure, empowering their teams to excel. A culture of ownership emerges. When accountability is modeled at the top, it cascades throughout the organization, fostering a sense of responsibility and initiative at all levels.

The Impact of Accountability on Team Morale

Accountable leadership does more than just improve performance; it builds stronger, more motivated teams.

Employees thrive in environments where:

- Leadership is transparent and consistent.
- Mistakes are viewed as learning opportunities rather than sources of punishment.
- Expectations and responsibilities are clearly communicated.
- Recognition is given to those who take initiative and demonstrate ownership.
- A leader's energy and mindset are positive.
- A vision of the future is inspiring and energizing.

When leaders utilize the nine-step framework, employees feel empowered to take responsibility for their work, knowing they are supported and guided rather than micromanaged or blamed. It provides a two-way conversation that is transparent. It provides the tools and develops the skills of accountable teams. It even makes it fun. "What step are we on right now?" are often conversations I hear between a manager and team member when it's done right. People also self-select that the team and job is not for them. When this happens, you know you have cultivated positive accountability. I've experienced many times when a team member opted to resign because they knew exactly what was expected and made the conscious decision that the job was not for them. When your team members make the decision willingly to resign and accept that they may not be the right person for the job it shows you've been clear, however understand that this means you have communicated step 2-4 exceptionally well. Sharing the consequences with someone makes them think about what they want to do next. When this step is missed it causes more confusion. So be ready to share with your team if you don't meet the expectation, or deliver on the goals, I will not be able to promote you, increase your pay, etc. be clear it helps people make the decision that is best for them which is ultimately best for the team.

A company's culture is shaped by the values and behaviors reinforced by leadership. When positive accountability is a core value, it becomes ingrained in the way teams operate. Organizations with a strong culture of accountability benefit from:

- Higher employee engagement. Employees feel more connected to their work when they **understand their role** in the company's success.

- Lower turnover rates. When people feel responsible for their work and supported in their growth, they are less likely to leave.
- Improved collaboration. Accountability encourages open communication and teamwork, as individuals understand how their contributions impact others.

Leadership's Influence on Individual Growth

Leaders play a pivotal role in the personal and professional growth of their teams. By holding themselves accountable and encouraging the same from their employees, they help individuals develop key skills such as: Self-discipline and time management. Employees learn to manage their responsibilities effectively.

- Problem-solving and critical thinking. When individuals take ownership of their work, they become more proactive in finding solutions.
- Resilience and adaptability. A culture of accountability encourages learning from failures rather than avoiding challenges.

- Curiosity, ideation and agency. Three skills that are essential to our future workforce.

Practical Steps to Reinforce Accountability in Leadership

Communicate Expectations Clearly

Set clear goals and responsibilities for each team member. Provide guidance and resources to ensure success. Ensure that your team understands the expectations, this is where most leaders go wrong they send out a memo, text, email but don't validate. A simple response to let me know you got this and understood is easy to add into emails, texts etc. Also asking at the end of a meeting for someone to recap top takeaways and next steps is such a powerful way for you, the leader, to validate that you've been clear. In our training you will see we use start, stop and continue to ensure team members validate their learnings. It opens up dialogue to validate understanding.

It is always very interesting to me at the end of a session what people will start, stop, and continue. It truly shows how each individual has understood and taken away what is important to them. And sometimes it's not what's important to you.

Foster a Positive mindset and Feedback Culture

Encourage regular check-ins and open discussions about performance.

Normalize constructive feedback and self-evaluation. Adopting fearless feedback and making it fact based is a good way to start. One of the critical prerequisites for a thriving culture of positive accountability is for leaders to open the lines of feedback both ways. Apple does this well. An easy template to achieve this is the WIN acronym. When this happens, people are able to say, "Here's what I need." This is such a powerful way to communicate and supports a positive way to give feedback. It keeps communication fact-based and non-accusatory. In case you have never heard of WIN before, it stands for WHEN this, It makes me feel, here's what I NEED. This is not a new concept but it is a powerful one, we teach this in conflict management training, it diffuses conflict and helps people receive feedback positively. As it is not using YOU statements which can be perceived as accusatory.

Recognize and Reward Accountability

Acknowledge employees who take ownership and exceed expectations. Create a system for peer recognition to reinforce positive behaviors. You can never say thank you enough. People love recognition, so make it fun, make it beneficial, and make it part of how you do business all the time. Every Friday, I set time aside to recognize someone. I called it "Follow-up Friday."

Encourage a Growth Mindset

Promote learning opportunities and development programs. Show employees that mistakes are part of the learning process. Celebrate them, do not shame them.

Lead by Example

Hold yourself to the same standards you expect from others. Admit mistakes and demonstrate how to take corrective action. Also remember: your team wants to work for a competent leader. So, if you are deficient in any way, put a plan in place to grow the skills your team needs you to have.

Transforming a Team Through Accountability

I have had the honor of leading teams for over three decades. I've also supported business owners and leaders over many years to build and deliver award winning customer experiences in a high turnover industry. Retail is a field where many people think it is impossible to retain staff and grow what seems to be impossible. Low traffic, ecomm, AI, worsening economy, and so many other factors are derailing to a business.

But none of the challenges can minimize the effect that happens when people feel valued. That is what your team wants. They also want clarity, a clear road map, and to work for someone who both cares for them and challenges them.

Even the advent of AI can't touch the power of connecting with your team. AI can never replace the human-to-human touch. No matter where technology goes in the future, people will always work for people, and high-performing people will always seek out and work for people who are high-performing.

If you are still wondering if accountability will work for you? I'd ask that you try it. Host a meeting with your team. Have each person complete the assessment we have provided for free. Then discuss your results together. This is a great way to start the process.

I'll never forget the day a senior executive I was coaching said to me, "April, can we tattoo this accountability wheel on our arms?"

I laughed because I knew exactly what he was saying. When it's adopted, it takes the mystery and fear away. It sets up a clear pathway to transform and gives you the filter to make great decisions. I say great decisions because we can all make good decisions, but the best leaders don't just make good ones; they make great ones.

Accountability in leadership is not just about achieving business results; it is about shaping a culture where people take ownership, feel valued, and contribute to a shared vision. By modeling positive accountability, you create a ripple effect that influences teams, business culture, and individual growth.

The question every leader should ask themselves is:

What kind of ripple effect am I creating today with my team, peers and customers?

Leadership is not defined by the title you hold but by the ripple you create. Positive accountability isn't a checklist; it's a mindset, a way of leading that brings out the best in others while holding yourself to the same standard. The leaders who transform teams are the ones who make accountability visible, who value people enough to challenge them, and who create clarity in the chaos.

As you close this book, remember this: every conversation you have, every expectation you set, and every assumption you reframe sends a ripple through your team, your culture, and your results. The choice is yours. Will your ripple be one of fear and confusion, or one of clarity, growth, and possibility?

Start today. Model positive accountability and watch your team and your leadership transform. Lead with clarity. Model accountability. Create ripples that last.

Acknowledgments

Writing this book has been a journey, and I am deeply grateful to the many individuals who have supported me along the way. I want to thank the leaders and teams who generously shared their experiences and insights, allowing me to weave real-world examples and case studies into this practical guide.

A special thank you goes to Angee Costa and my team. You continue to show up, inspire, and remind me why this work matters. We keep doing the work because of your belief, dedication, and unwavering support.

Appendix

This appendix includes supplemental materials to enhance your understanding and application of the nine-step framework for building an accountable culture.

Appendix A: Self-Assessment Questionnaire: A detailed questionnaire to assess your current leadership style and accountability practices.

Appendix B: Team Accountability Assessment Tool: A tool for evaluating your team's current level of accountability.

Appendix C: Constructive Feedback Template: A template for providing clear and constructive feedback to team members.

Appendix D: Conflict Resolution Strategies Checklist: A checklist to guide you through the conflict resolution process.

Glossary

Accountability: Taking ownership of one's actions, decisions, and outcomes, and being answerable for them. This goes beyond simply being responsible for tasks; it encompasses commitment to results.

Responsibility: Being assigned a task or duty.

Blame: Attributing fault or error to someone.

Psychological Safety: A shared belief held by team members that the team is safe for interpersonal risk-taking.

SMART Goals: Specific, Measurable, Achievable, Relevant, and Time-bound goals.

Growth Mindset: A belief that abilities and intelligence can be developed through dedication and hard work.

Fixed Mindset: A belief that abilities and intelligence are static and innate.

Appendix A: Self-Assessment Questionnaire

Evaluate your current leadership & accountability practices.

Instructions: Rate each statement from **1 (Strongly Disagree)** to **5 (Strongly Agree).**

1. I set clear expectations for my team.
2. I follow through consistently on commitments.
3. I welcome feedback, even when it's difficult.
4. I model the behaviors I expect from others.
5. I address underperformance directly and constructively.
6. I take responsibility for both successes and failures.
7. I coach my team regularly, not just during reviews.
8. I measure success by both results and team growth.

Scoring:

- **32–40:** Strong, consistent accountability leadership.

- **20–31:** Room to strengthen consistency and clarity.

- **Below 20:** Accountability practices need immediate focus.

Appendix B: Team Accountability Assessment Tool

Use with your team to measure current accountability levels.

Team Rating Scale (1–5): 1 = Rarely / Never

3 = Sometimes

5 = Always

Dimension	Key Question	Rating
Clarity	Does everyone know what success looks like?	
Ownership	Do team members take initiative without being told?	
Trust	Do teammates admit mistakes and share learnings?	
Feedback	Is feedback exchanged regularly and constructively?	
Results	Do we consistently meet agreed goals?	

Appendix C: Constructive Feedback Template

Guide for clear and actionable feedback conversations.

1. **Situation:** "When [specific behavior/action] happened..."

2. **Impact:** "...it resulted in [impact on team, customer, or results]."

3. **Expectation:** "What's needed is [desired behavior/standard]."

4. **Support:** "Here's how I can help you succeed..."

5. **Commitment:** "Can we agree to this next step?"

Tip: Keep feedback timely, factual, and focused on behavior, not personality.

Appendix D: Conflict Resolution Strategies Checklist

Steps to move through conflict productively.

☐ Define the issue clearly—separate facts from assumptions.

☐ Allow each party to share their perspective without interruption.

☐ Identify shared goals (e.g., team success, customer satisfaction).

☐ Explore options collaboratively before choosing a solution.

☐ Agree on clear actions and responsibilities.

☐ Follow up to ensure the agreement is honored.

☐ Reflect: What did we learn to prevent similar conflicts?

Author Biography

April Sabral is a highly sought-after leadership coach and consultant with thirty years of experience working with organizations of all sizes across various industries. She has a proven track record of helping leaders build high-performing, accountable teams. Her expertise lies in developing practical strategies for fostering a culture of accountability that drives results while improving employee morale and engagement. April holds a Bachelors in Metaphysics from the University of Sedona and is a certified WBAC, John C. Maxwell Trainer and The Positive Effect Transformational Leadership System. She is a frequent speaker at industry conferences and workshops, sharing her insights on leadership, accountability, and team dynamics. She is passionate about empowering leaders to create positive and productive work environments where individuals thrive and achieve their full potential

Improve your team's accountability.

To Invite April to speak to your team, contact April@AprilSabral.com

Did you find this book helpful? Leave a review on the site where you purchased it, it helps more leaders like you find the transformative power of Positive Accountability.

We will see you in a training soon!

www.ingramcontent.com/pod-product-compliance
Lightning Source LLC
Chambersburg PA
CBHW070917130626

46555CB00001B/172